The Accessible School

UNIVERSAL DESIGN FOR EDUCATIONAL SETTINGS

BY LAUREL BAR, M.S., OTR/L
AND JUDITH GALLUZZO, OTR/L

INSTRUCTIONAL DESIGNER
SUZANNE D. SINIFT, M.A.

MIG COMMUNICATIONS
BERKELEY, CALIFORNIA

Editors: David Driskell, Paul Yee, Leslie Barton
Cover and page design: MIG DesignWorks
Illustrator: Teresa Lehane

Library of Congress Cataloging-in-Publication Data
Bar, Laurel, date.
    The accessible school : universal design for educational
settings / by Laurel Bar and Judith Galluzzo ; instructional
designer, Suzanne Sinift.
        p.   cm.
    ISBN 0-944661-20-3 (pbk.)
    1. School buildings—Access for the physically handicapped—
United States.   2. School buildings—United States—Design
and construction.   I. Galluzzo, Judith, date.   II. Sinift,
Suzanne D., date.   III. Title.
LB3222.3.B26   1999
371.9'045—dc21   98-51671

MIG Communications
800 Hearst Avenue
Berkeley, CA 94710 USA
510/845-7549
510/845-8750 (fax)

Please note: None of the guidelines in this book should be interpreted as design standards or codes of any sort. They are provided as guidelines and suggestions only. It is your responsibility to ensure that your site and building are designed and constructed in accordance with applicable federal, state, and local codes and standards. Building design and construction are complex and subject to many legal constraints and requirements. DO NOT rely on this book to ensure legal or contractual compliance with any federal, state, or local laws. Consult the appropriate documents and officials in the jurisdiction in which your site is located.

table of contents

preface

The purpose of *The Accessible School* is to help designers, educators, and administrators understand how the physical environment can support human activities and to illustrate how this knowledge can be applied to educational facilities. The book was also developed to increase sensitivity to different levels of physical ability, locomotion, sensory awareness, and intellectual ability. A broad understanding of the concept of disability will help to ensure that everyone's needs are fully addressed.

Creating and maintaining school environments that accommodate a wide range of abilities can be extremely difficult. The key to meeting this challenge, we believe, lies in the principle of universal design.

We were introduced to universal design by Ron Mace, an architect, in 1989. As occupational therapists and consultants in accessible design, we wish to bring the qualities inherent in universal design—adaptability, safety, and cost-effectiveness—to educational settings. A Small Business Innovative Research Grant from the U.S. Department of Education afforded us the opportunity to write *The Accessible School*. The process has been a long but rewarding one, filled with a great number of individuals who have encouraged and inspired us, celebrated each milestone, bolstered our sagging spirits, and given sage advice. Among those who deserve special thanks are Suzanne Sinift, David Driskell, Leslie Barton, David Moffat, Paul Yee, Laurel Kelly, Arvid Osterberg, Judy Waterman, Elaine Ostroff and the Adaptive Environments Center staff, Robin Moore, Susan Goltsman, Nancy Lamport, Sue Lasoff, Robert Bar, and Gary Galluzzo.

We hope that this book will contribute to the development of school settings where the individual, not the environment, determines the level of participation, and where *abilities*, not disabilities, provide the focus of the educational process.

Laurel Bar, M.S., OTR/L
and Judith Galluzzo, OTR/L

universal access to education

The process of designing educational environments is a complicated and challenging one. It demands the careful consideration of a wide spectrum of issues, including the needs of the users, the school curriculum, fluctuations in student population, ongoing changes in technology, and practical considerations such as safety, maintenance, and energy conservation.

A recent trend in American education has added another layer of complexity to school design. Forced into action by legislation and fiscal realities, school districts across the country have reduced or even discontinued "special-education" programs and have begun integrating children with special needs into regular education classrooms. As a result of this shift in educational policy, a greater emphasis has been placed on the accessibility of school environments.

Accessibility in schools, in a strict legal sense, means that all students have the opportunity for equal education in the "least restrictive environment."[1] Obtaining true accessibility, though, requires more than simply installing a wheelchair ramp at the front entrance. Designers, educators, and facility managers alike must fully understand how the physical environment limits or enables human actions, as well as the diverse ability levels that must be accommodated. Comprehension of these ideas marks the first step toward achieving a truly accessible school. The desire to create settings that are the "least restrictive" to the widest range of users is the primary force behind universal design. The goal of universal design is an environment where everyone—regardless of ability or disability—can participate to the fullest extent. This comprehensive approach makes universal design particularly relevant in the design and management of educational settings, where an especially broad spectrum of ages, abilities, needs, and activities can be found.

Universal design is not a set of inflexible rules. Its proponents, while recognizing the value of standards such as the ADA Accessibility Guidelines, realize that compliance alone does not guarantee accessibility for all people. Instead, universal design focuses on the complicated interrelationships that exist between the physical environment and the users. Universal design incorporates the general principles of its predecessor, barrier-free design, which emphasized the removal of physical barriers and the creation of specially designed features for people with disabilities.[2] Unlike barrier-free design, however, universal design is not based on the assumption that wheelchair-accessible facilities are also accessible to individuals with other disabilities—for some people, barrier-free features can

---

[1] Individuals with Disabilities Education Act (IDEA) Public Law 101-476, originally known as the Education of All Handicapped Children Act of 1975.

[2] The first national directive regarding accessible design, issued by the Public Building Administration in 1959, reflected the barrier-free design approach: "All new Federal buildings shall provide easy access of wheelchairs to the first floor entrance lobby. Where entrance steps are unavoidable, ramps and handrails must be provided." (President's Committee 1959, in Steinfeld et al. 1978)

even be hazardous. Universal design avoids these limitations by incorporating a more comprehensive view of human needs and abilities.

Four commonly held goals in the universal design movement provide the basis of the guidelines in this book.

Accommodate human movement characteristics. Universal design addresses three aspects of human movement: body space, reach range, and effort. Body space represents the area immediately surrounding a person and any mobility aid she or he may use—in other words, the space needed to move through an environment. Accessible design requirements for clear space, such as vertical clearance and minimum passage width, address this need for maneuvering space. Reach range represents the distance users can reach to retrieve an object. These ranges are used to determine where items should be placed to be accessible. Effort represents the physical exertion required to perform a function such as flipping a switch or ascending a ramp. The required level of effort is determined by the dexterity (i.e., required degree of manipulation), force, and sequence of steps needed to perform the function.

Ensure safety. When facilities are designed to accommodate the way people work and move through their environments, obstructions and hazards are minimized. A well-designed pathway, for example, provides a smooth and secure path of travel for someone walking, using a wheelchair, or carrying a bulky item.

Provide adaptability. Facilities must be planned with both present and future needs in mind to accommodate constant changes in population, technology, and building regulations. Every aspect of a facility should be designed for maximum flexibility and use by the broadest spectrum of people.

Be cost-effective. Affordability and cost-effectiveness are valued in universal design. Expenses are reduced when designs accommodate the easy rearrangement, addition, or removal of structural elements rather than requiring constant retrofitting or renovation. Furthermore, the selection of products based on the general requirements of human movement eliminates the need to purchase costly specialized equipment. Lever-type door handles, for example, are not significantly more expensive than other types of handles yet they make doors easier to open for all users.

Universal design's basic principles of adaptability, diversity, and choice can provide solutions to the unique design challenges presented by educational settings. Its encompassing approach can help to foster a positive environment for learning—between teachers and students, among students, and between students and the environment.

User Groups

Successful universal design requires a thorough understanding of the potential users of a facility. The designers and managers of school settings are faced with a complicated set of challenges since the users of schools make up a particularly diverse group in terms of needs and abilities. A school population can be divided into the following five major user groups, although specific needs within a particular facility can vary and must be fully defined before initiating design development. Designers and managers should also note that these groups do not include the many people of all ages and abilities who attend athletic events, social gatherings, night classes, town meetings, election polls, and other activities held at school sites.

Students

Students themselves are a diverse group. Representing a wide age range, students spend their school years developing basic mental and physical skills. Since the rate of development varies for each child, learning environments must fit a broad range of abilities. Whether a space serves one grade level or the entire student body, designers must be aware of the different needs of children.

A student's physical, sensory, mental, and emotional abilities affect how he or she engages in classroom activities. Since the ability to participate can shape learning experiences and contribute to self-image and identity, educational spaces must be designed to facilitate these developmental processes.

Designers should strive to provide students of all ages and abilities with safe yet stimulating experiences both in and out of the classroom.

Teachers

Teachers need classroom settings that do not inhibit their ability to facilitate the educational process. Teachers must be able to move freely around the classroom, interact with students on an individual basis, and use instructional equipment with ease. Since teachers have individual needs based on their personal teaching style and physical abilities, it is doubly important that classrooms provide a basic level of accessibility and adaptability. As more students with special needs participate in classroom settings, teachers will need to broaden their educational goals and instructional methods. Flexibility is needed to meet the educational needs of each child while also allowing the class as a whole to accomplish its objectives.

Well-designed classrooms help all children to function independently, freeing the teacher to focus on educational goals.

Administrators

Administrators must ensure that all students have equal access to education in the least restrictive environment which is appropriate to their needs. While many administrators accommodate children with special needs by moving classes to first-floor rooms or arranging to transport wheelchair users up a flight of stairs, these solutions are only temporary and fail to remove the physical barriers to full participation in the learning environment. Facilities designed for free movement allow administrators to place students in classes based on educational goals and interests rather than logistical concerns such as room accessibility.

To protect school districts from potential liability, administrators must ensure that all buildings, whether newly constructed or retrofitted, meet all accessibility and safety standards. Administrators must also be careful not to discriminate against people with disabilities when overseeing employment policies and practices, as mandated by Title I of the Americans with Disabilities Act.

A universally designed facility that meets or exceeds ADA guidelines can better accommodate the needs of present and prospective users and will allow administrators to focus on educational issues.

Support Professionals

Support professionals, such as occupational and physical therapists and speech and language pathologists, provide individualized assistance to students with special needs. As part of their instruction, they often need to modify the work area to meet particular needs of the students. In adjustable environments, therapists and students can concentrate on educational goals rather than strategies for overcoming physical barriers. An adjustable computer desk, for example, can be easily raised to fit a student's wheelchair, enabling the therapist to focus on the child's computer skills, not his or her inability to reach the keyboard or see the screen.

Adjustable environments enhance the personalized instruction provided by support professionals.

Maintenance Personnel

Maintenance personnel are often involved in modifying educational facilities to meet new building standards and the changing needs of the school population. A flexible environment facilitates these design adjustments and minimizes maintenance costs. For example, an auditorium with removable seats interspersed throughout the room enables maintenance workers to adjust a section quickly to allow wheelchair users to sit with their classmates. Similarly, adjustable shelving enables staff workers to raise, lower, or remove shelves easily to meet changing storage needs.

Universally designed facilities allow greater efficiency in the use of time, effort, and services of the maintenance staff.

The Range of Abilities and "Disabilities"

Designers and managers of educational facilities should familiarize themselves with the range of human abilities and "disabilities." Terms such as "disability," "functional impairment," and "limitation" reveal very little about a person's actual level of ability. Disabilities vary widely in severity, and each person has a different degree of success in compensating for the functional effects of a disability. In fact, some people with disabilities can perform many functions better than individuals considered "able-bodied." Stereotypical views of people with disabilities can lead to environments that only serve a narrowly defined group of users.

Impairments to the following functional areas affect the development of children and should be considered when attempting to accommodate the full range of a student's abilities in a school environment:

- hearing
- vision
- mobility
- upper body functions
- strength and stamina
- proprioception and tactile senses
- brain function (specifically mental retardation).

Hearing

Hearing limitations range from slight hearing loss to profound deafness. Six categories are used to identify levels of hearing impairment: *slight, mild, moderate, moderately severe, severe,* and *profound.* Hearing loss is also categorized according to time of onset: *prelingual* hearing loss occurs before speech and language acquisition; *postlingual* hearing loss follows speech and language acquisition; and *prevocational* hearing loss occurs before the age of nineteen.

When the sense of hearing is nonfunctional, the person is diagnosed as deaf.

Causes. There are two main types of causes of hearing loss. *Conductive* hearing loss is caused by a mechanical difficulty in the conduction of sound through the middle ear, with the inner ear typically remaining undamaged. *Sensorineural* hearing loss is pathological, caused by a lesion in the inner ear or along the nerve pathway from the inner ear to the brain stem. *Mixed* hearing loss is a combination of conductive and sensorineural hearing loss.

Causes of hearing loss include infection, otitis media (fluid in the middle ear), otosclerosis, cerumen (earwax), brain injury resulting from trauma to the head, extreme environmental noise, Ménière's disease, emotional stress, drugs, and the aging process.

Results. Hearing loss results in limited and inaccurate communication and can seriously affect a child's mental, emotional, and educational development. A direct correlation exists between the age of onset and the severity of developmental delay or disability; the earlier in life a hearing loss occurs, the greater its effect on a person's language development. At any age, even a partial loss of hearing can cause a person to feel isolated. Measures to improve communication are essential to provide a comfortable environment that supports the full development of children with hearing impairments.

Vision

Visual impairments range in severity from the use of corrective lenses to complete blindness. Individuals with limited visual ability develop and rely upon other senses for information about the environment. Visual ability can be measured three ways: acuity, range, and perception.

Acuity is the quality of the visual image. Is the image clear with good contrast or does the visual field appear blurred, cloudy, or distorted?

Range is the field of vision. Limitations in range are defined as scotoma (peripheral vision remains

Common Types of Assistive Devices for Individuals with Hearing Limitations

Amplification Systems

Personal frequency modulated (FM) and Easy Listeners auditory trainers provide a direct communication link between teachers and students with hearing disabilities. The teacher wears a microphone and transmitter to communicate directly with the student via coupling techniques such as headphones, teleloops, or direct audio input into their personal hearing aids.

Classroom FM amplification systems allow teachers to use a microphone and transmitter to project their voice through speakers placed around the classroom.

Hearing aids are devices worn in the ear to amplify sounds. One drawback is that security systems with ultra-high frequency sounds, electric transformers with low-cycle frequency sounds, fluorescent lights, aquariums, computers, paging systems, and beepers can interfere with FM systems and hearing aids. The most common problem with wearing a hearing aid is cosmetic. Students and their parents often feel that by wearing a hearing aid the students will appear different from their peers.

Non-Auditory Signals

Flashing lights on alerting or signaling devices, such as telephones, alarm clocks, smoke detectors, and pagers, translate sound into a visual signal.

Vibration allows alerting or signaling devices to translate sound into a tactile signal.

Telecommunication Devices

Text telephones, such as telecommunication display devices (TDDs) and teletypewriters (TTYs), allow phone communication through typed messages. Voice Carry Over is a feature with TDD which allows students to use their own voice instead of typing a text. Trained operators are available through relay services to provide links between text telephones and voice-only phones.

Captioned video programming uses text to display dialogue and other sounds visually. Captioning is preferable to projecting interpreters in a corner of the screen, which can be distracting and hard to see. Closed captions (cc) are only visible with the use of a telecaption decoder. Open captions, which are always visible, are becoming more widely used.

Person-to-Person Communication

American Sign Language (ASL), the most common type of sign language used by deaf people in the United States within the deaf culture, is a visual-gesture language with its own semantic and syntactic structure. Some individuals communicate through Signed English, which involves the use of ASL in English syntax. Two other manual communication systems are Signed Exact English and Cued Speech.

---

clear but central vision is decreased), tunnel vision, (central vision remains clear but peripheral vision is decreased), and hemianopsia (half the visual field is affected, such as when the right field of vision is occluded).

Perception is the interpretation of visual information. For example, depth perception provides vital data about the relational distances of objects in the field of vision. People with impaired depth perception may find it difficult to walk down stairs because they cannot determine where one step ends and the next one begins. They may also find certain floor patterns challenging to walk across because some areas of the surface appear higher than others.

Causes. There are many causes and types of visual limitation, as illustrated in the following overview of visual pathology.

Refraction errors are the most common cause of visual impairment. Refraction errors are commonly called far-sightedness (hyperopia) or near-sightedness (myopia), conditions that occur when light entering the eye focuses behind (hyperopia) or in front (myopia) rather than directly on the retina. Another refraction error, astigmatism, occurs when rays of light entering the eye do not focus sharply on the retina but instead spread over a diffuse area, causing image distortion. Approximately 15 percent of the population suffers from serious refraction errors.

Common Types of Assistive Devices for Individuals with Vision Limitations

Corrective lenses. Glasses or contact lenses can often provide users with corrected vision. Although they do not provide a permanent solution to the loss of vision, they are effective in correcting aphakia and many refraction errors. Lens implants provide a more permanent replacement for lenses damaged by cataracts.

Alternative media. The use of large print enhances the ability of persons with low vision to read written information. Signs and printed materials are often available in Braille; however, not everyone who is blind or who has very limited visual ability reads Braille. Models and tactile maps are useful methods of communicating scale, size, and shape.

Auditory Devices

Recorded materials and computers. Traditionally, books-on-tape and other recorded educational materials were most commonly used as replacements for written materials for students with visual impairments. The introduction of computers into the classroom, however, particularly those with Braille keyboards, sound cards, and voice-activated functioning, has opened a world of possibilities for these students.

Auditory signals on alerting or signaling devices. Many cities have installed auditory signals at crosswalks. Similar signals could be useful on school campuses.

Movement Assistance Techniques

Canes. Some individuals with visual impairment use a cane while walking to check if the pathway is clear. Cane users are typically trained in two techniques.

A person using the touch technique moves the cane from side to side, touching points outside both shoulders. This method is useful in unfamiliar areas where objects in the vicinity may change position.

In more predictable and familiar environments, a person might use the diagonal technique in which the cane is held in a stationary diagonal position across the body. The tip of the cane touches or just hovers above the ground at a point outside one shoulder, with the handle or grip extending to a point outside the other shoulder. The cane acts as a shield against objects in front of the person, while the ends of the cane can detect objects on either side.

Guide dogs. An alternate mobility aid for individuals with a visual impairment is a seeing eye or guide dog. The presence of these specially trained dogs requires few design modifications beyond providing adequate clear floor space adjacent to seating.

Retinitis pigmentosa, a congenital disease of the retina that primarily affects male children, causes night blindness and progressive loss of peripheral vision. It can eventually result in tunnel vision or complete blindness.

Glaucoma (increased intraocular pressure behind the eyes) can cause optic nerve damage and decreasing peripheral vision, resulting in varying degrees of vision loss.

Corneal dystrophy is a genetic disease in which the cornea develops abnormally. One of the more common causes of corneal pathology, it blurs vision and makes eyes overly sensitive to light and easily irritated.

Aphakia results when a lens is absent, loose, or displaced, causing visual deficits in the affected eye.

Cataracts occur when lenses become opaque, causing images to appear cloudy, particularly when looking into bright reflected light.

Strabismus is an intermittent or constant deviation of the pupils that cannot be voluntarily controlled (i.e., the eyes do not move together or focus on the same object). This condition can cause ocular fatigue and impair vision when looking at close or distant objects. Most children with strabismus eventually learn to perceive depth and distance by using one eye at a time; a small percentage will lean their heads to the side or close one eye in an attempt to eliminate double vision. Esotropia is a form of strabismus more commonly known as "crossed eyes."

Trauma to the eyes can lead to many visual problems. A direct blow to the eye or a foreign body that contacts or penetrates the eye surface can cause infection or leave scars, impairing or even eliminating vision. Ninety percent of such injuries could be avoided if appropriate preventive measures are taken. The simple act of wearing protective eyewear when playing racquetball and many other sports can dramatically reduce the chances of serious injury.

Diabetes mellitus is a common cause of visual impairment, including blindness; in fact, diabetes is the leading cause of nontraumatic blindness in the United States. When diabetes is chronic (i.e., lasting more than five years), it may cause abnormalities in the small blood vessels in the eye, particularly those located in the retina. These abnormalities can lead to bleeding and scars that decrease visual acuity.

Brain damage, whether congenital or acquired, can cause cortical blindness, reduce the visual field, affect acuity, or distort visual perception.

Results. Even correctable vision abnormalities can have serious effects on children's physical or mental development. Very young children with impaired, but correctable, vision can be incorrectly labeled with functional blindness or mental retardation. Poor vision may prevent students from fully participating in group activities or classwork. Physical "defects," such as crossed eyes or squint-

ing, can have serious social consequences in the worlds of both children and adults.

Mobility

Although most people with restricted mobility are ambulant, they all experience some difficulty when moving through the environment due to poor balance, incoordination, or limited strength and stamina. These limitations can necessitate the occasional or full-time use of mobility aids.

Causes. Incoordination, poor balance, and low strength and stamina are caused by a number of genetic and biological factors: congenital conditions such as cerebral palsy and spina bifida; disease and damage to the nervous system from muscular dystrophy, Parkinson's disease, multiple sclerosis, or hemiplegia; spinal cord injuries resulting in paraplegia or quadriplegia; heart and respiratory problems; and physical changes associated with aging.

Results. People with impaired mobility performance can experience any one or more of the following conditions.

Incoordination. People with poor coordination have difficulty controlling and directing their extremities. They may exhibit an awkward gait, poor eye-hand coordination, slow reaction time, and visual impairment. In addition, incoordination can affect speech and other forms of communication, such as body language and signing.

Poor balance. Individuals with poor balance lack a sense of security or confidence as they move through space. Poor balance can inhibit motor performance and increase the risk of falling.

Limited strength and stamina. People with limited strength and stamina tire easily and become short of breath quickly. They find it difficult to walk long distances or perform many other forms of physical activity, especially climbing steep stairs or ramps.

Decreased sensory stimulation. Children are particularly affected by the barriers to sensory experience that are imposed by mobility limitations. As children move through the environment, they receive tactile, vestibular, auditory, and visual stimulations that contribute to their neurodevelopment. Children with mobility limitations, however, experience decreased sensory stimulation from such movement.

Reliance on mobility aids. The use of mobility aids such as crutches, walkers, canes, and braces can cause an unsteady gait and make negotiating steep gradients extremely difficult. Adequate clear floor space is critical for people using mobility aids; additional maneuvering space for mobility aid usage must be considered when determining personal space requirements.

Common Types of Mobility Aids

Crutches. The use of crutches significantly impedes mobility and speed. Stairways and other changes in grade can be extremely difficult and hazardous for people using crutches. Activities that require significant use of the hands, such as opening and closing doors, are particularly challenging because the hands must be used for stability and support on the crutches. People using crutches also require considerable space to the front and sides to allow for safe mobility and maneuvering.

Walkers. People using walkers move in a slow, straightforward direction. The fixed, rectangular shape of a walker often requires additional clear width at aisles, doorways, and passageways, especially when the person makes a turn or other maneuver. Adequate clear floor space also must be available to allow the person to place the walker securely on the floor ahead of them when making forward progress.

Canes. Canes are useful for people with a wide range of visual and mobility limitations. A cane used to provide balance and stability requires less clearance than the longer cane used by a person who is blind.

Braces. People wearing braces may also use crutches, walkers, or canes. The additional weight of leg braces can further limit a person's stamina.

Wheelchairs/Motorized Vehicles. Wheelchair users exhibit a wide range of abilities. Some individuals possess good upper body strength and can propel themselves independently, while others need to be pushed or must use an electric wheelchair or motorized vehicle. When designing an accessible environment several issues must be considered: the type of disability, the extremities involved, the amount and type of muscle function, and the size of the wheelchair and its user. These factors determine the reach ranges, clearances, and other dimensions associated with providing accessibility.

Upper Body Functions

Limits to upper body functioning are often caused by the inability to use one or both hands or arms and can involve the use of a prosthesis.

Causes. Conditions that cause limitations in arm and hand functions include diseases of the joints, muscles, and nerves; amputations; broken bones; developmental malformations; high muscle tone; low muscle tone; and short stature. The use of mobility aids, such as crutches or canes, can also limit upper body functions and motion.

Results. Limitations in hand and arm functions can result in muscular weakness, poor coordination, limited reach, or lack of dexterity. Functional ability is affected in a variety of ways. A daily activity such as dressing requires coordination and sufficient range of motion in the arm to pull on a shirt, dexterity to button a shirt, and strength throughout the dressing process. Actions such as coloring or writing require dexterity, upper extremity coordination, and hand, arm, and trunk strength.

Strength and Stamina

Shortness of breath can decrease the supply of oxygen to the body and cause muscle weakness, thereby decreasing a person's strength and stamina. This limitation can range from feeling weak and dizzy with physical exertion to the inability to walk even a short distance. These conditions may require the use of supplementary oxygen and/or a motorized vehicle or electric wheelchair.

Causes. Common conditions that decrease strength and stamina include: disorders that cause shortness of breath, such as respiratory conditions (for example, asthma, allergies, and sinusitis) and pulmonary diseases (for example, emphysema); neurological diseases such as multiple sclerosis; cardiovascular disorders such as severe hypertension; use of a lower extremity prosthesis or brace; side effects of certain medications; post-surgery convalescence; pain; and the aging process.

Results. For people with limited strength and decreased stamina, a small amount of physical exertion can result in extreme fatigue, dizziness, or shortness of breath. Most stationary activities should be performed in a seated position. Standing is aggressively avoided. Travel is often difficult and must be limited to short distances. Paths and walking routes are often chosen for the availability of resting places and the absence of hills or a flight of stairs. Frequently, walking aids such as canes or walkers are used to provide support for short distances; wheelchairs are used for longer distances.

Proprioception and Tactile Senses

Sensory loss varies widely in extensiveness and severity. Sensory loss can completely or partially affect a portion or all of the body, including one or both sides of the body, one or both arms or legs, or parts of one arm or leg. Sensory loss can affect both deep and superficial sensory input, which the body reads, interprets, and responds to through three categories of sensory function.

Exteroceptive (superficial) sensation results from receptors located in the skin and relays information to the brain regarding pain, heat, cold, pressure, and touch. An exteroceptive sensory deficit reduces or eliminates the body's instinctual responses to such potentially dangerous stimuli as excessive heat and sharp objects.

Proprioceptive (deep) sensation sends information to the brain regarding the body's movement and its position in space. The nervous system receptors, located in the muscles, tendons, joints, and labyrinths of the inner ear, initially receive this information and then transfer it to the brain. Disturbed or absent proprioception will result in sensory-motor disabilities.

Stereognostic sensation is the combination of proprioceptive and exteroceptive sensations. It provides the brain with information about the characteristics of three-dimensional objects (for example, texture, shape, and size) gathered by touching and handling the object. The ability to reach into one's pocket and select a quarter rather than a dime is the result of stereognostic sensation. A reduction or loss in stereognostic sensation can prevent a person from perceiving an object's physical characteristics by means of touch.

Causes. Common conditions that cause limitations in kinesthetic and tactile sensation include: spinal cord injuries resulting in paraplegia or quadriplegia; stroke or other cerebrovascular accidents; brain damage such as cerebral palsy; head injuries resulting in hemiplegia; neurological conditions such as pinched nerves or cumulative trauma; and neurological diseases such as multiple sclerosis.

Results. The most common sensory loss is *hypesthesia*, a diminished sense of pain, heat, cold, pressure, or touch. This sensory feedback is a critical protective body mechanism that alerts the brain to potential danger or injury. When this type of feedback is inadequate or unavailable, the body must place greater reliance on auditory and visual senses. However, no matter how highly these senses are developed, they do not provide adequate protection from environmental dangers. The loss of sensory feedback, or even a delayed perception of sensory stimuli, can result in severe injury from hot, sharp, or rough surfaces.

In contrast to hypesthesia, *hypersensitivity* to tactile stimuli can cause an increased motor reaction. For example, children with hypersensitivity may overreact to being touched, thus becoming hyperactive, or they may find light touch, such as tickling, more unsettling than a hug. Also, they often find touching themselves less upsetting than having others touch them.

Sensory feedback guides body movements. Without accurate sensory feedback, many motor skills can be impaired, including mobility and dexterity. The ability to walk on an uneven surface, for example, depends on accurate feedback to translate the condition of one foot being higher than the other in order to make an appropriate physical adjustment. Lack of sensory feedback can also impair fine motor manipulation. Even a person with an intact sensory system may experience a delay in perception that results in slow reaction time and incoordination.

Good handwriting requires both deep and superficial sensory input and controlled movement. A student with adequate motor control may still find handwriting extremely difficult if there is inadequate sensory feedback. Students who have a difficult time with handwriting can opt to use a word processor but may still be frustrated by the hand movements required for typing. Effective typing requires both the knowledge of where one's fingers are without looking at the keyboard (stereognostic sensation) and the ability to feel pressure exerted on the keys (superficial sensation). Writing and typing require the ability to stop one motor impulse and substitute a diametrically opposed action. For example, writing requires smooth and rapid direction changes to form a variety of letters. This ability, called *diadochokinesis*, depends on sensory input.

A person who experiences a decrease in the automatic movements of hands or limbs, for whatever reason, must increasingly rely on visual feedback to control movements. Simple tasks such as brushing teeth, finding an item in a pocket, or tucking in a shirt require visual attention and concentration. If negative experiences increase, the person may become too discouraged to attempt even simple tasks.

Mental Retardation

While recognizing that "mental retardation" is not a desirable term, the American Association on Mental Retardation (AAMR) continues its use in the absence of a more universally recognizable term. Since 1988 the AAMR's Ad Hoc Committee on Classification and Terminology has been researching and developing a new definition of mental retardation, which focuses on the functional level of a person as he or she interacts with the environment, and in 1992 they published a revised definition.

Mental retardation refers to substantial limitations in present functioning. It is characterized by significantly subaverage intellectual functioning, existing concurrently with related limitations in two or more of the following applicable adaptive skill areas: communication, self-care, home living, social skills, community use, self-direction, health and safety, functional academics, leisure, and work. Mental retardation manifests before age 18.

(Mental Retardation: Definition, Classification, and Systems of Supports; Washington, D.C.: American Association on Mental Retardation, 1992).

In other words, a person is considered mentally retarded if his or her IQ scores are 75 or below and if he or she displays limitations in two or more adaptive skill areas before the age of eighteen.

Causes. Historically, mental retardation was thought to be the result of either genetic influences or psychosocial disadvantage. This idea has been revised recently, since it has been estimated that 50 percent of people with mental retardation exhibit more than one factor that causes their disability. In addition, causal factors for mental retardation are difficult to separate because a disability often results from a combination of events occurring over time.

AAMR cites two "directions" of factors that are pertinent to the cause of mental retardation. The first direction describes types of factors, including biomedical, social, behavioral, and educational factors. The second direction identifies the timing of

Broadening the Concept of Mental Retardation

AAMR has developed a three-step process to diagnose and address the needs of individuals who have been screened for mental retardation. This process is intended to "broaden the conceptualization of mental retardation, to avoid reliance on IQ scores, to assign a level of disability, and to relate the person's needs to the intensities of supports necessary to enhance the person's independence/interdependence, productivity, and community integration." Its purpose is to eliminate use of categorical terms and, instead, focus on the abilities and needs of each individual.

The first step is the diagnosis of mental retardation, using AAMR's revised definition.

The second step is to identify an individual's strengths and weaknesses in relation to four dimensions: intellectual functions and adaptive skills (for example, education); psychological and emotional considerations; physical, health, and etiological considerations; and, finally, environmental considerations such as home, school, leisure, community, and work.

The third step is to assign the essential level of support based on strengths and weaknesses: intermittent (support available when necessary); limited (consistent, short-term involvement); extensive (regular, daily intervention); and pervasive (daily support for each dimension). One example of such a diagnosis for an individual who is mentally retarded might be "a person who needs intermittent support in self-care and extensive support in communication." Implicit in this diagnosis is the assumption that providing an appropriate level of support will enhance this individual's development.

the causal factor (or factors) to determine whether the person with mental retardation was directly affected and/or indirectly affected through his or her parents. Together, these directions are used to describe the causes of mental retardation.

Results. Mental retardation results in a generalized delay in a child's development. The Individuals with Disabilities Education Act (IDEA) and regulations in many states make children diagnosed with a "developmental delay" eligible for special-education services, which can begin as early as birth and, in most school districts, will continue through age twenty-one. As these students leave school and enter adulthood, they must have appropriate systems of support based on their level of retardation. An individual may be self-sufficient or live in a minimally supervised group home and work in a supervised setting. Adults in need of additional support often require closer supervision in residential and work settings. Supported employment, supported living, and regular-class support systems in education are testimony to the belief that these services, when appropriately assigned, can dramatically improve an individual's abilities and level of participation in society.

A Brief Legislative History of Accessibility

Accessibility was first brought to national attention in 1919 when the United States Congress authorized a vocational rehabilitation program for veterans who became disabled during World War I. Subsequent federal acts have helped to define accessibility and establish the fundamental civil rights of people with disabilities, a process that has culminated in the passage of the Americans with Disabilities Act of 1990. The following legislative summary provides the legal context for current mainstreaming efforts and the development of universal design.

American National Standards Institute

ANSI A117.1 Standard. The ANSI A117.1 Standard was the first building standard to address accessibility directly. Since its initial release in 1961, ANSI A117.1 has been considerably revised and expanded. The standards are reviewed every five years by a committee of more than fifty organizations representing individuals with disabilities, rehabilitation professionals, designers, builders, manufacturers, and governmental agencies. The private sector, in general, has accepted the 1980, 1986, and 1992 versions of ANSI A117.1. The current edition of the ANSI standard (redesignated CABO/ANSI 117.1-1992) has been adopted by all of the model building codes in the United States.

Architectural Barriers Act of 1968

Public Law 90-480. The Architectural Barriers Act created the first federal law requiring facility access for people with physical disabilities, stating that "any building or facility constructed in whole or in part by federal funds must be made accessible and usable by the physically handicapped." The act, though fairly limited in scope (affecting only federally funded construction or renovation projects), had a profound impact. It provided the legislative mandate for the development of accessibility standards and the legal foundation for future accessibility efforts, including the Americans with Disabilities Act.

Uniform Federal Accessibility Standards (UFAS)

Federal Standard 795. Established in 1984, UFAS defines the standards for design, construction, and alteration of buildings to meet the requirements of the Architectural Barriers Act. UFAS references the ANSI A117.1 Standard and is based on the Minimum Guidelines and Requirements for Accessible Design (MGRAD). MGRAD was developed in 1982 by the Architectural and Transportation Barriers Compliance Board to provide direction to federal agencies that oversee federally owned, leased, or financed buildings. Buildings and sites that require public access, or that might serve as a place of employment for a person with disabilities, are among the facilities addressed in these standards. UFAS, however, does not address program accessibility issues except as they relate to physical access.

Rehabilitation Act of 1973; Title V, Section 504

Public Law 93-112, amended by PL 516 and PL 95-602. Unlike the Architectural Barriers Act, which addresses only physical access to facilities, Section 504 of the Rehabilitation Act addresses the issue of barrier-free programming by requiring that people with disabilities have access to federally assisted programs. The manner in which agencies meet the requirements of the Rehabilitation Act is left to their discretion. The act simply states, "No otherwise qualified handicapped individual in the United States . . . shall, solely by reason of handicap, be excluded from the participation in, be denied the benefits of, or be subjected to discrimination under any program or activity receiving Federal financial assistance." For example, if a wheelchair user enrolls in a federally funded course held on the third floor of a non-accessible building, the facility must be made accessible or the class must be moved to an accessible site. The course need not be held in an accessible classroom at all times, but there must be a plan in place for making it accessible when the need arises.

Individuals with Disabilities Education Act (IDEA)

Public Law 101-476. IDEA, originally known as the Education of All Handicapped Children Act of 1975, greatly expanded the educational opportunities for children with disabilities. The law states that free, appropriate education for all children must be provided in the "least restrictive environment." The "least restrictive environment" clause implies that, unless there are special circumstances, children with disabilities should receive their educational services in a mainstream setting. In addition, each child is entitled to an Individualized Education Program (IEP); special education and related services; and mediation and due process. An IEP is an annual statement of goals and objectives for a child and is established by the school's support staff and the child's teacher and parents.

Americans with Disabilities Act of 1990 (ADA)

Public Law 101-336. The ADA is a comprehensive law prohibiting discrimination against people with disabilities in employment, public transportation, telecommunications, and public accommodations. It provides civil rights protection similar to that guaranteed to people on the basis of race, sex, national origin, and religion by the Civil Rights Act of 1964. The ADA extends the requirements of the Architectural Barriers Act to cover all facilities used by the general public, regardless of federal funding (for example, restaurants, hospitals, movie theaters, medical and law offices, and retail stores). These issues of physical accessibility are addressed in Title II (public services and public transportation) and Title III (public accommodations and services). Guidelines for implementation of the ADA were published in the *Federal Register* of July 26, 1991 (28 CFR Part 36, covering nondiscrimination on the basis of disability in public accommodations and commercial facilities) and September 6, 1991 (49 CFR Parts 27, 37, and 38, covering transportation facilities). These guidelines, known as the ADA Accessibility Guidelines (ADAAG), provide direction for those who must ensure accessibility in public facilities rather than providing a set of building codes.

Currently, the U.S. Department of Justice is proposing to amend ADAAG by adding a special application section for children's facilities to its Standards for Accessible Design. The proposed rules were published in the *Federal Register* of July 22, 1996 (28 CFR Part 38 and 36 CFR Part 1191). This new section will ensure that "newly constructed and altered children's facilities are readily accessible to and usable by children with disabilities."

State Laws. Some states have adopted building codes that go above and beyond the guidelines set forth in UFAS and ADAAG. Adherence to federal guidelines as well as relevant state codes must occur in these states when designing or evaluating accessible sites and buildings. In cases of inconsistency or overlap between federal guidelines and state codes, the more stringent standard must be applied. In states without specific building codes addressing accessibility issues, UFAS and ADAAG apply.

Staying Informed

Anyone involved in the design or management of schools should obtain a copy of the ADA Accessibility Guidelines (ADAAG) and applicable state and local codes. It is equally important to keep informed of changes in the content or meaning of accessibility laws. It may also be helpful to seek legal counsel when reviewing accessibility requirements and their implications.

For ADA information on the web:

http://www.usdoj.gov/crt/ada/

For ADA information on titles 2 and 3 or for a copy of ADAAG:

ADA Hotline
U.S. Department of Justice
Office of ADA
P.O. Box 66738
Washington, D.C. 20035-9998
(202) 514-0301 (voice and fax order number)
(202) 514-0383 (TDD)
http://www.usdoj.gov/crt/ada/adahoml.htm

For answers to questions regarding design standards and for supplementary information on the proposed ADA accessibility guidelines for children's facilities, contact:

Architectural and Transportation Barriers
    Compliance Board/Access Board
1331 F Street, NW, Suite 1000
Washington, D.C. 20004-1111
(800) USA-ABLE (voice/TDD)
(202) 272-5434 (voice/TDD)
(202) 272-5447 (fax)
http://www.access-board.gov

general dimensions

Accessibility design guidelines are frequently based on the anthropometrics (i.e., human body sizes and proportions) of adult wheelchair users, who typically have the greatest space requirements. Children usually possess less strength and have less mature coordination skills than do most adult wheelchair users. Children often experience more difficulty using mobility aids and require additional maneuvering space. They are also shorter than most adults, which further limits their ability to reach or see certain objects. As a result, a different set of dimensions needs to be applied when designing environments for children.

The ADA Accessibility Guidelines (ADAAG), which present design parameters for creating accessible facilities, should be understood and applied within the context of children's anthropometrics and the unique aspects of educational settings. Such special circumstances are addressed by the "equivalent facilitation" provision of ADAAG 2.2, which states that departures "from particular technical and scoping requirements of this guideline by the use of other designs and tech-

nologies are permitted where the alternative designs and technologies used will provide substantially equivalent or greater access to and usability of the facility."

Using ADAAG as a foundation, the following chapters present guidelines that incorporate the anthropometrics of children, which are based on a study conducted by the Center for Accessible Housing (CAH) at North Carolina State University. Their findings, used by the Architectural and Transportation Barriers Compliance Board to modify UFAS for application in children's environments, were published in a 1992 report entitled *Recommendations for Accessibility Standards for Children's Environments*. CAH recommendations that provide the basis for a guideline in this book are referenced appropriately. In addition, the special application section for children's facilities, currently under consideration by the U.S. Department of Justice and the Access Board (1996), was consulted in determining the guidelines presented in this book. In general, the proposed rule changes are intended to cover facilities that are constructed according to children's

dimensions and anthropometrics for ages two through twelve (ADAAG, Children's Facilities, 15.1 and A15.1). Most states apply design standards based on adult dimensions and sizes for children's facilities serving those over twelve years of age.

All guidelines—whether quoted directly from ADAAG or adapted to meet the needs of children—must be applied within the context of applicable federal, state, and local building codes; fire, plumbing, electrical, and structural codes; and other related requirements. In addition, the consultation of a design professional with experience in accessible design is essential. Since each facility presents a unique set of design challenges, the appropriate response cannot always be determined solely on the information provided in this book.

Section II presents many basic space requirements of adults and children, particularly those of wheelchair and cane users. These measurements provide guidelines for designing spaces or elements not specifically addressed in federal, state, or local guidelines and regulations.

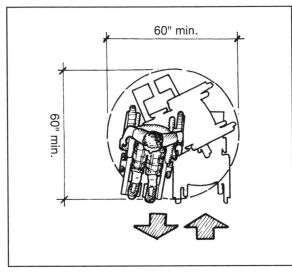

Figure 2-1

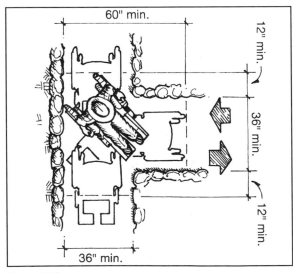

Figure 2-2

Space Allowances

Accessible elements and areas within a school facility depend on the availability of sufficient space to enable users to travel freely and to operate equipment independently. Given the crowded conditions in many school settings, space allowances also provide a measure of safety.

Clear Passage Width for Child Wheelchair Users. Child wheelchair users require a minimum clear width of 44 inches (1120 mm) in all passageways (CAH 4.2.1). When it is anticipated that more than one child will be using a passageway simultaneously, the recommended clear width is 88 inches (2235 mm), which allows two child wheelchair users to pass one another safely (CAH 4.2.2). State building and life safety codes generally require hallways or corridors to be wider than 44 inches (1120 mm), so this passage width requirement should have little cost and space impact in the design of school hallways or corridors. The Access Board is currently considering a proposed rule change to require a 44-inch (1120 mm) width for interior and exterior accessible routes.

Clear Passage Width for Adult Wheelchair Users. Adult wheelchair users require a minimum clear width of 36 inches (915 mm) in all passageways. This width provides enough space for individuals to propel manual wheelchairs without bumping their knuckles against a wall. This clear width may be reduced to 32 inches (815 mm) for a distance no greater than 24 inches (610 mm) (for example, the width of a doorway) (ADAAG 4.2.1).

When it is anticipated that more than one person will be using a passageway at the same time, the clear width should be expanded to allow for passing. A minimum clear width of 48 inches (1220 mm) allows an adult wheelchair user and an ambulatory person to pass. The minimum clear width required for two wheelchair users to pass is 60 inches (1525 mm); comfortable, unconstricted flow, however, requires a clear width of 64 inches (1625 mm) (ADAAG 4.2.2, A4.2.1[3]).

Wheelchair Turning Space. Wheelchair users require clear space at the end of accessible routes to make 180-degree turns. Turning space should also be provided at points where individuals may decide to change course, such as at intersections between corridors, wings, and activity areas.

When making 180-degree turns, wheelchair users typically use one of two methods, depending on the turning space available. The easier method is the pivot turn, which requires a circular turning space measuring 60 inches (1525 mm) in diameter (Figure 2-1). The second method, which is more cumbersome and time consuming, involves multiple forward and backward motions within a T-shaped intersection of two corridors, each measuring

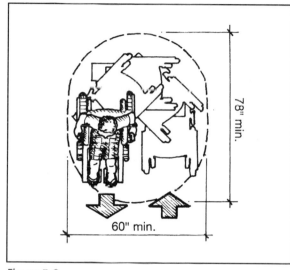

Figure 2-3

36 inches (915 mm) wide and 60 inches (1525 mm) long (Figure 2-2) (ADAAG 4.2.3). The required wheelchair turning spaces for both methods are the same for children and adults.

However, to ensure that wheelchair users can make smooth 180-degree turns without repeated tries or bumping into objects, turning spaces should measure at least 60 inches (1525 mm) wide by 78 inches (1965 mm) long (Figure 2-3) (ADAAG A4.2.3).

Clear Floor Space for Wheelchair Users. Child and adult wheelchair users require an approach allowance of at least 30 inches (760 mm) wide by 48 inches (1220 mm) long of clear floor space to access

stationary objects such as drinking fountains, desks, and public telephones. Clear floor space may be configured to accommodate either a side or forward approach (Figures 2-4 and 2-5) and may include up to 19 inches (485 mm) of the clear knee space required underneath items such as desks and sinks (ADAAG 4.2.4.1). CAH recommendations, based on the less-developed upper-body strength and maneuvering skills of children, suggest that an approach width of 36 inches (915 mm) is more appropriate in children's environments. The proposed rule changes to ADAAG include increasing clear floor and knee clearance width to 36 inches (915 mm).

One complete, unobstructed side of the clear floor space must adjoin or overlap an accessible route or another clear floor space. If the clear floor space is located in an alcove or otherwise confined on all or part of three sides, additional maneuvering space may be required. For instance, when a wheelchair user approaches an alcove from the side and the clear floor space extends more than 15 inches (380 mm) into the alcove, an additional 12 inches (305 mm) of maneuvering clearance is required (Figure 2-6). When approaching a clear floor space from the front, which extends more than 24 inches (610 mm) into the alcove, a wheelchair user requires an additional 6 inches (150 mm) of maneuvering clearance (Figure 2-7) (ADAAG 4.2.4.2).

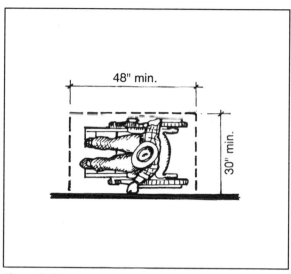

Figure 2-4

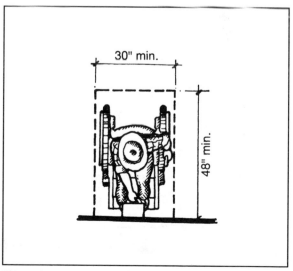

Figure 2-5

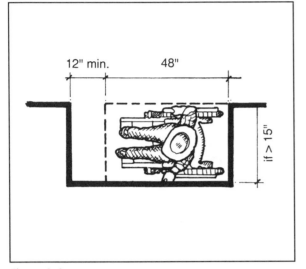

Figure 2-6

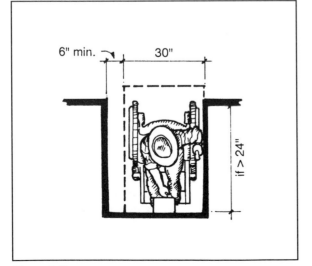

Figure 2-7

Reach Ranges for Wheelchair Users

The distances adults and children can reach to retrieve or use an object vary considerably depending on whether they are standing or using a wheelchair. For items to be considered accessible, they must be placed within a wheelchair user's reach range, which is also dependent on whether a side or forward reaching motion must be used. When wheelchair users have sufficient clear floor space available to make a parallel approach, they can use a side reach, which has a slightly larger range than a forward reach. If the space configuration only allows retrieval or use of the object from a forward-facing position, then wheelchair users must use the more restrictive forward reach.

Reach Ranges for Child Wheelchair Users. When child wheelchair users must reach from either the side or the front, CAH has recommended that objects be placed between 20 and 36 inches (510 and 915 mm) above the floor (Figure 2-8) (CAH 4.2.5–6). The proposed rule changes to ADAAG include more specific high and low reach range guidelines based on the age of the intended users (ADAAG, Children's Facilities, 15.2.1 and 15.2.2).

These revised reach ranges are intended to apply only to those controls, operating mechanisms and storage elements designed specifically for use

TABLE 2-1 FORWARD AND SIDE REACH RANGES FOR CHILDREN		
AGES	HIGH	LOW
2 through 4	36 inches (915 mm)	20 inches (510 mm)
5 through 8	40 inches (1015 mm)	18 inches (455 mm)
9 through 12	44 inches (1120 mm)	16 inches (405 mm)

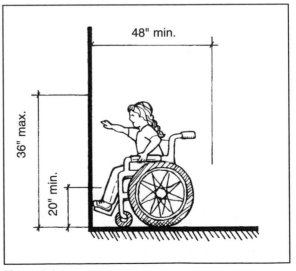

Figure 2-8

by children. Elements provided for use by adults are covered by regulations that are outlined below.

Side Reach Range for Adult Wheelchair Users. When adult wheelchair users reach from the side, objects must be placed between 9 and 54 inches (230 and 1370 mm) above the floor (Figure 2-9)—unless the reach extends over an obstruction more than 10 inches (255 mm) deep (for example, a countertop). If such an obstruction does not measure more than 34 inches (865 mm) above the floor or more than 24 inches (610 mm) deep, objects may be placed on it, but not higher than 46 inches (1170 mm) above the floor (Figure 2-10) (ADAAG 4.2.6).

Forward Reach Range for Adult Wheelchair Users. When adult wheelchair users reach forward, objects must be placed between 15 and 48 inches (380 and 1220 mm) above the floor (Figure 2-11) (ADAAG 4.2.5). As is the case for side reach ranges, these dimensions only apply when there is no obstruction (for example, a desktop). If an obstruction measures less than 20 inches (510 mm) deep with clear floor space underneath that is as deep as the obstruction itself, then objects may be placed on it, but not higher than 48 inches (1220 mm) above the floor (Figure 2-12). For wider obstructions—those between 20 and 25 inches deep (510 and 635 mm)—with clear floor space underneath that is as deep as the obstruction itself, the

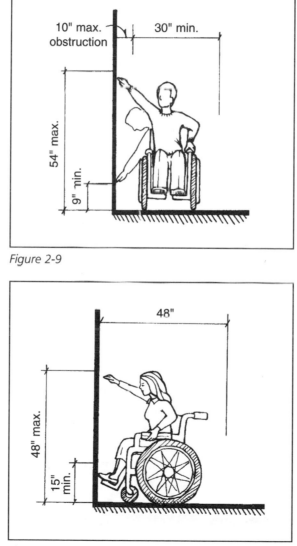

Figure 2-9

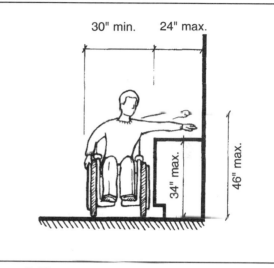

Figure 2-10

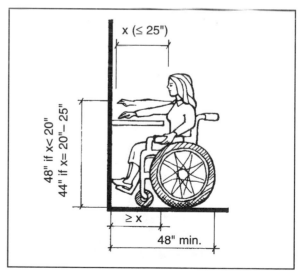

Figure 2-11

Figure 2-12

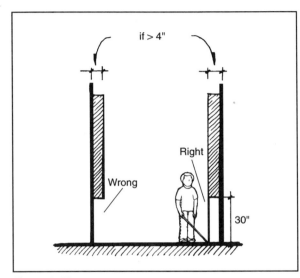

Figure 2-13

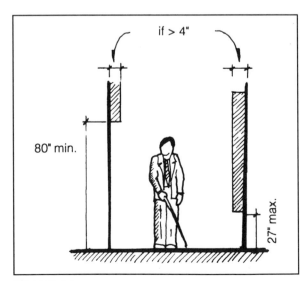

Figure 2-14

reach range narrows to 44 inches (1120 mm) above the floor. Any obstruction more than 25 inches (635 mm) deep will prevent access to objects.

Protruding Objects

Objects that project into a pathway or maneuvering space can create safety hazards and accessibility barriers. Protruding objects are particularly common in school settings, where trash cans, telephone banks, drinking fountains, vending machines, and display cases line heavily used corridors. Although protruding objects may not appear obstructive, they can be as limiting as a locked door if they reduce the clear width of passageways to less than 32 inches (815 mm).

Guidelines for protruding objects are based on the cane detection range of people with visual impairments. When cane users cannot detect a protruding object mounted above the ground, they may accidentally bump into it and injure themselves. As a result, two aspects of protruding objects must be considered: the height at which the object is placed and the distance that it projects from a wall. In general, the lower an item is placed, the farther it can project. A protruding object, however, may never reduce the required clear width of a passageway or maneuvering space.

Safe Dimensions of Wall-Mounted Objects for Children. More stringent requirements for protruding objects are recommended for environments used by children, since children have a shorter stride and a different cane detection range than do most adults. CAH guidelines recommend that objects that protrude 4 inches (100 mm) or more from the wall should extend to the floor (CAH 4.4.1). The proposed rule changes to ADAAG would allow such protruding objects to be mounted with their leading edges no higher than 12 inches (305 mm) from the floor (reduced from the current requirement of 27 inches [685 mm]) (ADAAG, Children's Facilities, 15.3). Objects less than 30 inches (762 mm) high that project between 1 and 4 inches (25 and 100 mm) from the wall should, however, extend to the floor (Figure 2-13) (CAH 4.4.1).

Safe Dimensions of Wall-Mounted Objects for Adults. Most adults using a cane will detect a protruding object whose lowest edge is no higher than 27 inches (685 mm) above the floor. Thus, protruding objects whose lowest edge occurs at or below this height may project any distance from the wall in environments not intended for use primarily by children. Items with their lowest edge between 27 and 80 inches (685 and 2030 mm) above the floor must not project more than 4 inches (100 mm) from the wall (Figure 2-14) (ADAAG 4.4.1).

Freestanding Objects. Post-mounted objects between 27 and 80 inches (685 and 2030 mm) above the ground may overhang up to 12 inches (305 mm) in environments not intended for use primarily by children (ADAAG 4.4.1). The proposed rule changes to ADAAG would require that the leading edge of a post-mounted object with a 12-inch (305 mm) overhang must also be mounted no more than 12 inches (305 mm) above the floor in children's facilities. In no case should protruding objects reduce the clear width of an accessible maneuvering space.

Vertical Clearance

People with limited vision or those who pay insufficient attention to their surroundings can be injured by low-hanging objects such as signs and light fixtures. As a result, all pathways, aisles, and other areas of circulation must have a minimum vertical clearance of 80 inches (2030 mm) from the floor or ground (ADAAG 4.4.2).

Areas that adjoin accessible routes must have a minimum vertical clearance of 80 inches (2030 mm) or contain a barrier that blocks access (ADAAG 4.4.2). For example, a display case could be positioned to prevent people from walking into an area with restricted headroom.

Controls and Operating Mechanisms

Many elements in a school facility, such as light switches, lockers, vending machines, and soap dispensers, require the manipulation of controls and operating mechanisms. Universal use of these mechanisms depends upon careful placement and choice in design.

Heights for Children. The controls and operating mechanisms of equipment intended for use by children should be located within the reach range of child wheelchair users. Whether side or forward reach is used, controls and operating mechanisms should be located at heights appropriate for the age group of the intended users (see Table 2-1, page 18).

Heights for Adults. The controls and operating mechanisms of equipment intended for use by adults should be located within the reach range of adult wheelchair users. When side reach is used, controls and operating mechanisms must be located between 9 and 54 inches (230 and 1370 mm) above the floor. When forward reach is used, they must be located between 15 and 48 inches (380 and 1220 mm) above the floor (ADAAG 4.27.3).

Operation. All controls and operating mechanisms must be operable with one hand. They must require neither an excess of 5 lbf (22.2 N) nor tight grasping, pinching, or twisting of the wrist (ADAAG 4.27.4). Since children generally possess less strength than adults, controls and operating mechanisms intended for their use should require no more than 3 lbf (13.3 N) (CAH 4.27.4). Ideally, controls and operating mechanisms should be operable with the closed fist of either an adult or child. Such accessible mechanisms include lever handles, push bars, push buttons, and slide controls.

Labels. To assist people with low visual ability, labels explaining the method of operation (such as "on" and "off") should be printed using large, raised letters or symbols in colors that have a contrast of at least 70 percent against their background.

site accessibility

Every day, individuals—on foot or bicycles and in cars, buses, vans, and trucks—arrive at school sites during congested periods. Such congestion presents special challenges to the designer of routes in and around an educational facility. Safety and accessibility must be primary concerns, with special attention given to efficient traffic flow.

This section outlines basic design guidelines for the outdoor areas of a school site. The creation of well-planned approaches, entrances, and outdoor environments will help to provide a friendly, safe, and inviting atmosphere for all.

Vehicle Access

Roads

Roads around and within a school site should be designed to discourage speeding and encourage a smooth flow of traffic. Streets should be clearly marked and well lit. The surface material should be stable and non-slippery when wet, particularly at pedestrian crosswalks.

Traffic Flow. Several types of vehicles must access a school site, each with a different purpose: school buses and passenger cars drop off or pick up children at loading zones; faculty, staff, and student cars park in designated areas; and maintenance and delivery vehicles provide services essential to a school's operation. Whenever possible, provide separate routes for each group to minimize congestion. Each traffic route should be clearly visible to pedestrians; confusing, poorly defined routes can be dangerous for pedestrians trying to cross them.

Speed Control. Although reduced speed limits for designated school zones on public streets are often posted, they are not always enforced. Through proper design and management, however, the probability of serious accidents can be reduced. School officials and designers should work with local traffic engineers to address the problems of speed control and traffic flow. Tactics to increase safety include textured pavement, speed bumps, or choke-downs (i.e., extending the sidewalk into the parking lane). More radical design alternatives

include modifying vehicular routes by forcing traffic to slow down and veer to the left or right. Flashing lights and signs (preferably stop signs) also play an important role in alerting motorists to the presence of school children.

Bike Paths. Bike paths should be installed next to the sidewalks leading to schools. They should have a level surface and be well lit, with signs and pavement markings that clearly identify them.

School Loading Zones

Loading zones provide areas for passengers to safely enter and exit a vehicle. During peak periods, school loading zones can become congested with cars, buses, and waiting children. To ensure safety and accessibility, they must be well planned and properly located to keep vehicular traffic from interfering with pedestrian or bike routes. Passenger vehicles should travel to and away from the loading zone by means of a circular or drive-through route without having to back up after loading or unloading.

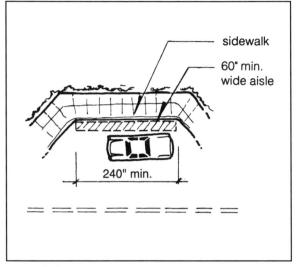

Figure 3-1

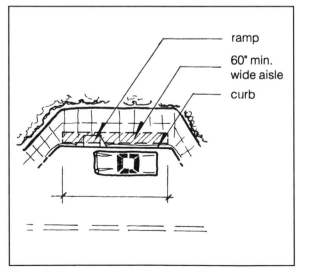

Figure 3-2

When more than one loading zone is provided, at least one must be accessible (ADAAG 4.1.2[5][c]). An accessible loading zone consists of space for a vehicle to pull up and an access aisle with sufficient space to enter or exit a vehicle for people using mobility aids (Figure 3-1).

Access Aisles. Access aisles must be level and located directly adjacent and parallel to the area where vehicles pull up. Generally, these aisles must measure at least 5 feet (1.5 m) wide and 20 feet (6 m) long (ADAAG 4.6.6). Those in school loading zones, which experience heavy traffic volumes, must be substantially larger. In addition, most children need more time to board or exit a vehicle than adults. Access aisles used primarily by children should measure at least 12 feet (4 m) wide and 50 feet (15 m) long (CAH 4.6.5). If any access aisle is located on a different level than the pull-up space, a curb ramp must be provided (Figure 3-2) (see Curb Ramps in this section).

Waiting Areas. Waiting areas at school loading zones should include benches with backrests and arm supports. Benches benefit every member of a school's population, but they are essential for those with poor mobility, limited strength, or decreased stamina.

To provide shade and protection from inclement weather, accessible loading zones should be covered. This cover should measure at least 20 feet (6 m) long and should extend at least 6 feet (2 m) over the vehicle pull-up lane (CAH 4.6.7).

Vertical Clearance. From the school site entrance to the accessible loading zone, the entire traffic route must have a minimum vertical clearance of 114 inches (2895 mm) (ADAAG 4.6.5), although at least 180 inches (4570 mm) is recommended to accommodate school buses and other large vehicles (CAH 4.6.6). The minimum clearance allows the passage of vans modified for people with disabilities.

Signage. Accessible passenger loading zones must be identified with a sign bearing the International Symbol of Accessibility (see Signage under Parking Areas) (ADAAG 4.1.2[7][b]).

Parking Areas

The entire route from the entrance to the parking areas must also have a minimum vertical clearance of 114 inches (2895 mm) (ADAAG 4.6.5).

Accessible parking spaces reserved for people with disabilities are required by law. An accessible parking space consists of a space for the vehicle and an adjacent access aisle to provide additional room for people using mobility aids to board or exit a vehicle. Two essential factors govern the design of accessible parking spaces: location and size. Accessible parking spaces must be located as closely as possible to the accessible route and accessible building entrances (ADAAG 4.6.2). Proximity of accessible parking to a facility is particularly important for people with low stamina, who may find excessive distances overwhelming or even prohibitive. If two or more accessible entrances exist, accessible spaces should be dispersed to serve each accessible entrance. In cases where a parking area does not serve a particular building, accessible spaces should be located as closely as possible to the accessible pedestrian route that connects the parking area to the main building entrance (ADAAG 4.6.2).

TABLE 3-1

TOTAL SPACES	ACCESSIBLE SPACES
1 to 25	1
26 to 50	2
51 to 75	3
76 to 100	4
101 to 150	5
151 to 200	6
201 to 300	7
301 to 400	8
401 to 500	9
501 to 1000	2 percent of total
1001 or more	20 plus 1 for each 100 over 1000

Accessible parking spaces must have adequate space to ensure accessibility for all users. Separate sets of dimensions apply to accessible parking spaces for cars and vans. Vans, which often use side-operating wheelchair lifts, require more space than cars. Universal parking spaces are so named because they accommodate both types of vehicles.

Number of Accessible Spaces. Use Table 3-1 to determine the minimum number of accessible spaces required for parking areas of different sizes (ADAAG 4.1.2[5][a]). If a site has more than one parking area, the number of required accessible spaces for the entire site may be divided unequally among areas if an equivalent or greater level of accessibility is ensured. One of every eight accessible spaces, but at least one, must be accessible to vans (ADAAG 4.1.2[5][b]). Parking lot designers should review local and state codes for variances in these requirements.

Dimensions. Accessible parking spaces for cars and vans must measure at least 96 inches (2440 mm) wide (Figure 3-3) (ADAAG 4.6.3). Local or state codes should be consulted for standards on the required length of parking spaces.

Access aisles must measure at least 60 inches (1525 mm) wide for car parking spaces and at least 96 inches (2440 mm) for van parking spaces. An access aisle in a parking area may not use a ramp; it

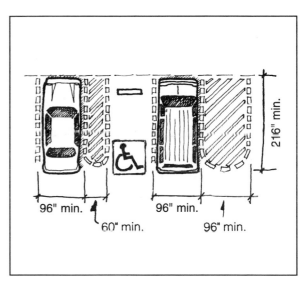

Figure 3-3

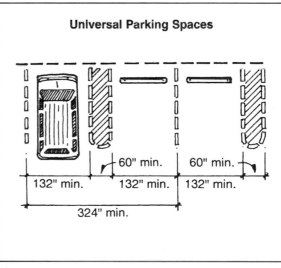

Figure 3-4

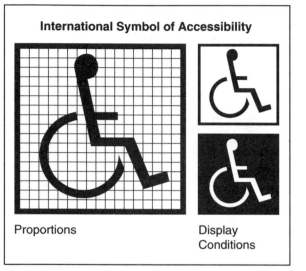

International Symbol of Accessibility

Proportions   Display
                     Conditions

Figure 3-5

required clear width

Figure 3-6

must be on the same level as its accessible parking space. Access aisles must be part of an accessible route that connects the parking area with the facility entrance (ADAAG 4.6.3). As a space-saving measure, two accessible parking spaces may share a common access aisle. Also, a van-accessible space and its access aisle at the end of a row may utilize otherwise unused space (ADAAG A4.6.3). Parked vehicles, planters, or other barriers may not obstruct an access aisle.

Universal parking spaces accommodate both cars and vans. They measure 132 inches (3550 mm) wide, with access aisles 60 inches (1525 mm) wide (Figure 3-4). This design eliminates the competition between car and van drivers for accessible parking spaces and the need for "Van Accessible" signs (ADAAG A4.6.3).

Slope. All accessible parking spaces and access aisles must have a slope of less than 2 percent (1:50) (ADAAG 4.6.3).

Signage. Each accessible parking space must be designated as reserved with a sign bearing the International Symbol of Accessibility (Figure 3-5) (ADAAG 4.6.4), and a "Van Accessible" sign mounted below to distinguish the larger parking spaces. Although this additional sign alerts van drivers to the availability of a wider access aisle, these spaces are not restricted to vans. All signs must be located so they cannot be obscured by parked vehi-

cles (ADAAG 4.6.4). To ensure visibility, signs should be positioned so that their bottom edge is at least 80 inches (2030 mm) above the ground; alternatively, signs may be mounted on a wall at a height of 36 inches (915 mm) above the ground.

Bumper Overhang. Bumpers of parked vehicles must not overhang onto an accessible route and reduce the minimum clear width of the path (Figure 3-6) (ADAAG 4.6.3). Bumper overhang can be prevented by placing a wheelstop, railing, or bollard along the edge of the adjoining walk. Continuous wheelstops are not recommended because they create tripping hazards and accessibility barriers; at least 36 inches (915 mm) should separate all barriers. Without wheelstops, railings, or bollards, the width of adjacent walkways must be increased by 36 inches (915 mm) to allow for bumper overhang.

Lighting. For safety and security reasons, all parts of a parking area should be well lit during evening hours.

Pedestrian Access

Accessible Routes

For a pedestrian route to be considered the site's accessible route, it must form a continuous unobstructed path that links the accessible elements of a building or facility and provides each user with independent access. The accessible route can consist of a variety of pathways, including side walks, corridors, aisles, skywalks, and tunnels (ADAAG 4.3.1).

In general, accessible routes should be designed to minimize travel distances to all points on the school grounds. Sites with significant slopes and differences in elevation may require a longer route along level terrain to meet accessibility requirements. For safety reasons, primary pedestrian paths of travel should be kept away from driveways and loading docks. Appropriate signage and physical barriers will discourage users from entering hazardous areas.

Newly constructed accessible sites must meet the following minimum requirements.

- The site must contain at least one accessible route that connects bus stops, accessible parking spaces, passenger loading zones, and public streets or sidewalks leading to an accessible entrance.

- At least one accessible route must connect accessible buildings, elements, and areas on the same site.

- All objects that project into the accessible route must meet guidelines for protruding objects and must not reduce the required minimum clear width (see Protruding Objects in Section II).

- Ground surfaces along accessible routes and in accessible spaces must comply with ADA guidelines (see Surface Material below) (ADAAG 4.1.2[1–4]).

Clear Width.   The accessible route must meet the minimum requirements for clear width for passageways (see Clear Passage Width in Section II).

Passing Space.   Wheelchair passing spaces are required if an accessible route has a clear width of less than 60 inches (1525 mm). For accessible routes used by children, wheelchair passing spaces measuring at least 74 inches (1880 mm) wide should be provided at intervals of no more than 100 feet (30 m) (CAH 4.3.4).

Passing spaces measuring 60 by 60 inches (1525 by 1525 mm) must be provided at intervals of no more than 200 feet (61 m) on routes intended primarily for use by adults. A T-shaped intersection of two corridors or pathways may serve as a passing space (ADAAG 4.3.4).

Surface Material.   The surface of an accessible route must be stable, firm, and slip-resistant (ADAAG 4.3.6). Concrete or asphalt can provide a smooth, secure surface. Brick or other unit pavers are also appropriate surface materials, so long as they are set in a level, concrete base and maintained regularly to ensure a level surface. The following

materials should not be used because they make an unstable surface and are prone to irregularities in height: flagstone, cobblestone, wood rounds, loose-laid brick, exposed aggregate concrete, earth, gravel, crushed stone, bark, and stone chips.

Changes in the color and texture of surface materials can serve as an orientation aid for people with visual limitations. Warning curbs are required when the accessible route drops off at its edge. If a walk is not separated from traffic lanes by means of curbs or other barriers, a detectable warning strip must be provided. Openings in gratings on a walking surface should not be wider than 1/2 inch (13 mm) in one direction. They should be placed perpendicular to the predominant direction of travel to minimize the likelihood of wheels falling into them (Figure 3-7) (ADAAG 4.5.4).

Slope.   The surface of an accessible route must not have significant level changes. Changes in level of greater than 1/4 inch (6 mm) up to 1/2 inch (13 mm) must be beveled. Changes greater than 1/2 inch (13 mm) must be accomplished by means of a short curb ramp, a longer ramp with a slope that does not exceed 1:12, an elevator, or a platform lift (ADAAG 4.3.6). An accessible route with a running slope greater than 1:20 is considered a ramp and should comply with the ADA guidelines for ramps (see Ramps in Section IV) (ADAAG 4.3.7). Since cross

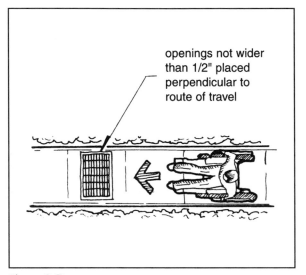

openings not wider
than 1/2" placed
perpendicular to
route of travel

Figure 3-7

slopes pose difficulties for wheelchair users, they must not exceed 1:50.

Doors. All doors included in an accessible route must be accessible (see Doors in Section IV) (ADAAG 4.1.3[7][c]).

Maintenance. Paths must always be kept clear of debris, ice, and snow because slippery or littered walkways are barriers for many people. Items should not be placed along the pathway, even on a temporary basis, if they will obstruct pedestrian access.

Temporary Route Changes. Appropriate signs are essential when a temporary change of route becomes necessary. People with mobility limitations or low stamina will need to plan for the longer distance imposed by the change. Those with visual limitations who rely on familiar landmarks for guidance may not be aware of hazards along the new route. Finally, those individuals who are not familiar with the school grounds must depend on signage to guide them to their destinations.

Crosswalks

Crosswalks should be visible to motorists and pedestrians at all times. Parking lots and loading zones should not be located where stopped vehicles will block sightlines between drivers and pedestrians trying to cross the street. Choke-downs improve visibility for pedestrians by allowing them to move past the parking lane before entering a crosswalk. Choke-downs also reduce the street-crossing distance. They are a signal that motorists should slow down and watch for pedestrians crossing the street. Crosswalks are an integral component of the pedestrian route of travel; to be effective in preventing jaywalking and promoting safety, they must be placed at all important intersections.

Crosswalk Markings. Crosswalks should be clearly labeled. Bold, yellow, slip-resistant paint should be used on the pavement to designate cross-walks. A warning sign should alert motorists that they are approaching a crosswalk, with another sign at the crosswalk itself. Informational signs should be placed along pedestrian routes to indicate the location of crosswalks and the presence of oncoming traffic. Signs intended for children should be placed perpendicular to the path of travel and at an appropriate height—48 inches (1220 mm) to the centerline, according to CAH recommendations, although the Access Board is currently investigating if another height—such as 42 inches (1065 mm)—would be more appropriate.

Crosswalk Signals. Besides traffic signal lights, visual and audio crossing signals should be provided at all crosswalks adjacent to school grounds. Visual signals should be bold, easy to understand, and placed so that they are visible to young children. Accompanying audio signals should consist of an intermittent whistling sound.

Curb Ramps

Curb ramps are short ramps that have a slope not exceeding 1:12, and are either recessed into or built up to a sidewalk curb. These ramps are important elements in accessibility design, enabling wheelchair users to travel easily between sidewalks and streets. Without proper design, however, curb ramps pose potential safety hazards. For example, wheelchair users can injure themselves if they accidentally roll off the side of a built-up ramp. A curb ramp on a street corner can misdirect a person with visual limitation into the middle of a busy intersection. A curb ramp must be slip-resistant, and it must contrast with the surface of the adjacent sidewalk. Well-designed curb ramps can make a site accessible to everyone—from those using a wheelchair to those gliding by on rollerblades or simply walking on foot.

Location. Curb ramps must be provided wherever an accessible route crosses a curb (ADAAG 4.7.1), such as at crosswalks, street intersections, and parking areas. Curb ramps must be positioned so that parked vehicles will not block them. At marked crossings, curb ramps must be contained completely within the markings (except for the flared edges of recessed ramps) (ADAAG 4.7.9).

Design Options. Allowable design options for curb ramps depend largely on location.

- A recessed curb ramp without returned curbs, or a built-up curb, in locations where pedestrians must travel across them, can have flared sides with a slope no greater than 1:10 (Figure 3-8). If the landing at the top of either type of curb ramp is less than 48 inches (1220 mm) deep (measured parallel to the direction of the ramp), the slope of its flared sides must not exceed 1:12 (ADAAG 4.7.5).

- If a curb ramp is located where pedestrians usually would not travel across it, returned curbs may be used (Figure 3-9) (ADAAG 4.7.5).

- Built-up curb ramps, which incline from the sidewalk down to the adjacent surface, may only be used if they do not project into lanes of vehicular traffic. The sides of built-up ramps must have a downward slope that does not exceed 1:10 (ADAAG 4.7.6).

- The design criteria for diagonal (or corner-type) curb ramps are complex. The flow of pedestrian traffic, street markings, and presence of flared sides can all influence the design. Refer to the ADA guidelines for more details (ADAAG 4.7.10).

Slope. The slope of curb ramps must meet the guidelines for the slope of accessible ramps (see Ramps in Section IV). The transitions from curb ramps to walks, gutters, or streets must be smooth and free of abrupt changes. The slopes of adjoining surfaces must not exceed 1:20 (ADAAG 4.7.2).

Width. Curb ramps, except those with flared sides, must measure at least 36 inches (915 mm) wide to accommodate wheelchair users (ADAAG 4.7.3). Those with flared sides must have at least 48 level inches (1220 mm) perpendicular to the route of travel (not including the sides).

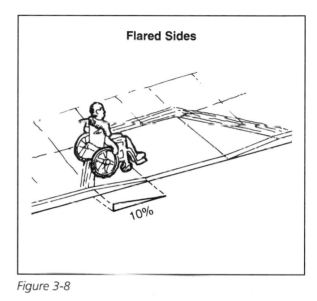

Flared Sides

10%

Figure 3-8

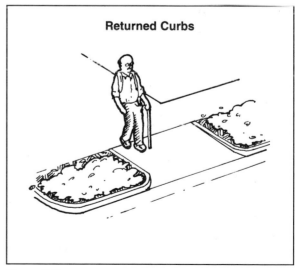

Returned Curbs

Figure 3-9

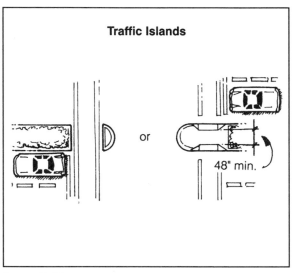

Traffic Islands

Figure 3-10

Traffic Islands. The pedestrian crossing at a raised traffic island must be accessible to wheelchair users. Accessibility is achieved either by providing a level cut through the island or placing curb ramps on both sides with a level area between them (Figure 3-10). If curb ramps are used, this level area must measure at least 48 inches (1220 mm) long, a distance that provides a safe place for wheelchair users to wait and rest (ADAAG 4.7.11).

Exterior Elements

The site design of an accessible school encompasses many more elements than buildings and the vehicular and pedestrian routes that serve them. Every aspect of a school site should promote learning in the broadest sense. Outdoor classrooms, learning labs, and play areas all contribute to a child's education, and the design of each should maximize educational opportunities.

The following guidelines focus on several specific aspects of physical accessibility in a school's outdoor environment. For a broader understanding of the many educational opportunities possible in a school, school designers and managers are encouraged to consult other sources, including *Play For All Guidelines*, 2nd edition (Moore, Goltsman, and Iacofano, 1992) and *Natural Learning: The Life History of an Environmental Schoolyard* (Moore and Wong, 1997). Those interested in a more general discussion of accessibility in outdoor environments are encouraged to consult *Universal Access to Outdoor Recreation: A Design Guide* (PLAE, 1993).

Landscape Buffers

Beyond aesthetic or educational considerations, the use of plants has great value in a school setting. Landscape buffers, for instance, can be used to separate pedestrian and vehicular traffic. They provide a safety zone for pedestrians and an area for the placement of signs.

Edged Walkways. When a wheelchair slips from a walk onto a grassy area, the situation is virtually impossible to correct without the help and concerted effort of others. This situation can be avoided by installing raised edging along wide walkways. Edging at least 4 inches (100 mm) high is adequate to keep wheelchairs from slipping off a walk. If a walkway has a drop-off greater than 4 inches (100 mm) at its side, a warning curb at least 6 inches (150 mm) high must be used. Edges on narrow walkways should have a beveled edge with a 30 percent slope where the curb meets the walkway.

Barriers. People with limited vision may not easily distinguish barriers along the edges of landscaped areas. For example, chains should not be used because they are difficult to see or locate with a long cane.

Signage. Signs located in landscaped areas should be posted in an individual's line of vision. However, since not everyone's line of vision is the same, it is good practice to consider a range of viewing heights that includes those for children, wheelchair users, and standing adults. People must be able to see signs readily, particularly at crosswalks.

Site Furniture

Site furniture such as benches, drinking fountains, telephones, trash receptacles, and other amenities should be located next to walks. Turnouts with benches and a parking place for a wheelchair provide convenient rest areas and meeting points. Site furniture should be accessible to all potential users.

Identification. Areas where site furniture is located can be distinguished by a change in ground material or color to alert people with visual limitations.

Surface Material. Site furniture should be located on a concrete or asphalt surface that is smooth yet slip-resistant. Brick and other unit pavers should be set in a level, concrete base. Concrete should have a "broom finish" surface (see Surface Material under Accessible Routes).

Protruding Objects. Protruding objects such as freestanding telephones, signposts, and plantings must be located so that they not reduce the clear width of an accessible route or maneuvering space (see Protruding Objects in Section II).

Seating. Seating with an adjacent clear space at least 36 inches (915 mm) wide for wheelchair users should be provided in shaded locations. A clear space of at least 18 inches (455 mm) in front of benches will ensure adequate space for people to sit comfortably without obstructing the path of travel.

Waste Receptacles. Open waste receptacles or those operable with one hand are preferred to foot-operated receptacles or those requiring two hands to operate.

Green Areas

Green areas on school grounds are designed to provide space for play, socialization, or other learning experiences.

Surface Material. The ground in open fields or play areas should be firm, smooth, and stable. An accessible route must lead to at least one of each different type of play event, sports field, or court.

Seating. Benches should be provided, as well as a shaded or semi-enclosed area to escape sun, wind, or inclement weather.

Vegetation. Vegetation on school grounds should be durable and easy to maintain. Plants with thorns or poisonous foliage must not be used. Trees should be planted at least 36 to 48 inches (915 to 1220 mm) from the walkway. Branches that hang below 80 inches (2030 mm) must be pruned, since they can be dangerous for people with limited or no vision ability. Dead trees, limbs, and plant material that can fall during strong winds should also be removed periodically.

Earth Berms. Earth berms can be used to define space, reduce the noise level by absorbing background noise, or provide raised seating. They should not be more than 36 inches (915 mm) high, so a person sitting nearby can see over them.

Exterior Lighting

The purpose of lighting at the school site is to increase safety and security and to provide illumination for evening activities. Good lighting requires a sufficient number of fixtures located in strategic locations. A lighting engineer should be consulted in this aspect of facility design.

Location. Sufficient exterior lighting should be located in the following places:

- Driveway entrances
- Parking lots
- Transit stops
- Accessible routes, circulation routes, crosswalks, and curb ramps
- Entrances to buildings
- Loading zones
- Locations where there are abrupt changes in grade or level.

Safety in Outdoor Play and Learning Environments

Accessibility and safety must share equal importance in the design of outdoor play and learning environments. Federal guidelines for safety in children's play environments are very complex and must be carefully followed. A design professional should be consulted to ensure that all federal, state, and local safety requirements are met when designing new facilities. Current issues in federal accessibility guidelines are discussed in Recommendations for Accessibility Guidelines: Recreational Facilities and Outdoor Developed Areas (Recreation Advisory Committee, developed for the U.S. Architectural and Transportation Barriers Compliance Board, July 1994). The American Society for Testing and Materials has developed a set of safety guidelines for playground equipment and surfacing. *Safety First Checklist*, 2nd edition (McIntyre and Goltsman, 1997) is a good resource for determining the safety and accessibility of existing facilities.

building accessibility

This section provides guidelines for the design of building elements that assist people in accessing different parts of a facility. It also covers general elements of school design.

Entering and Exiting the Building

Accessible Entrances

Accessible entrances are an essential component of an accessible school—they connect all users to the school's accessible path of travel, which must provide access to all primary areas of the school. Primary entrances are the first elements of a facility to greet site users. When these entrances are accessible, they help to create an inclusive atmosphere. Non-accessible entrances, on the other hand, send a negative message to all people with disabilities. Designers should take steps to ensure that all entrances are accessible. However, when secondary entrances cannot be made accessible, alternate routes must be readily available. The approach to the main entrance should be level and visible from the street. An easily identified

entrance will ensure that visitors enter at one location, thereby enhancing school security.

Number of Accessible Entrances. At least half of all public entrances to new facilities must be accessible. The number of accessible entrances must also be equal to or greater than the number of exits required by applicable building or fire codes (ADAAG 4.1.3[8][a]). Since emergency exits must be provided near all areas of buildings, it is strongly recommended that every new entrance be accessible.

When any existing entrance is altered, it should be made accessible to the greatest extent possible (ADAAG A4.1.6[1][h]).

Signage. In facilities where not all entrances are accessible, the International Symbol of Accessibility must be used to identify accessible entrances. At non-accessible entrances, signs directing people to the nearest accessible entrance must be posted (ADAAG 4.1.3[8][d], 4.1.6[1][h]). Directional signs should be located so that people will not need to

backtrack and waste precious energy to reach the nearest accessible entrance (see Signage under Moving through the Building).

Lighting. People with visual limitations may have difficulty adjusting between indoor and outdoor environments when outdoor light is strong and indoor lighting levels are relatively low. Some individuals may even become disoriented or experience temporary loss of vision. The placement of adequate lighting at all entrances will help people to gradually adjust to different levels of light.

Weather Protection. Recessing an entrance or providing a canopy or overhang will protect people and the walkway surface during inclement weather.

Stairs

Stairways in school settings can become highly congested areas, with many children running up and down the steps without paying attention to their footing. During times of peak activity, individuals who have difficulty negotiating stairs are at a distinct disadvantage. As a result, stairs must be designed and maintained with safety in mind. Slip-resistant surfaces, ample lighting, and routine removal of debris are recommended safety measures. Furthermore, alternate methods of access—such as ramps, elevators, or graded entries—must be provided for people unable to use stairs.

Only stairs between levels not otherwise connected by a ramp, elevator, or other accessible means of vertical access need to comply with ADA guidelines. However, since all stairs are potential hazards, compliance will help to ensure a safe environment for all users.

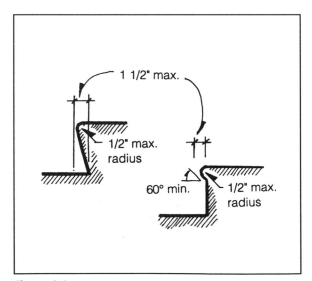

Figure 4-1

Treads and Risers. All of the steps in a staircase must have the same design, because variations in dimensions can disrupt a person's stride and cause tripping. In most settings treads must be at least 11 inches (280 mm) wide, measured from riser to riser. Open risers are prohibited (ADAAG 4.9.2).

Nosings. Individuals with limited ankle flexibility, such as people with leg braces or lower extremity prostheses, can catch their toes on a nosing and trip. As a result, nosings should not protrude, overhang, or have abrupt or square configurations. Nosings must meet the following guidelines:

- No abrupt undersides
- Curvature radius of 1/2 inch (13 mm) or less at the edge of a tread
- Sloped risers, or nosings with undersides angled 60 degrees or more from horizontal
- No nosings that project more than 1-1/2 inches (38 mm) (Figure 4-1) (ADAAG 4.9.3).

Stairwells. Stairwells should be enclosed or barriers should be installed to prevent people from inadvertently walking under them and bumping their heads (see Protruding Objects in Section II).

Outdoor Stairways. Although most safety requirements for interior and exterior stairways are identical, special attention must be given to exterior pathways, which are particularly haz-

ardous during inclement weather. Outdoor stairways and their approaches must be designed so that water will not accumulate on the walking surface (ADAAG 4.9.6).

Handrails. Accessible stairs must have continuous handrails on both sides of the pathway. The inside handrail of switchback or dogleg stairs also must be continuous (Figure 4-2) (ADAAG 4.9.4[1]). In order to prevent hand injuries, gripping surfaces must not be interrupted by newel posts, construction elements, or other obstructions (ADAAG 4.9.4[4]). Handrails must not rotate within their fittings, since such movement might cause a person's hand to "roll" off and decrease the sense of security (ADAAG 4.9.4[7]).

Handrail Width. Proposed rule changes for children's facilities would require that the gripping surfaces of handrails have a diameter or width of 1 to 1-1/4 inches (25 to 30 mm) (ADAAG, Children's Facilities, 15.4.2).

The diameter of rounded handrails for use by adults must measure between 1-1/4 and 1-1/2 inches (32 to 38 mm) in diameter (Figure 4-3). Other handrail shapes are allowed if they provide an equivalent gripping surface (ADAAG 4.26.2).

Handrail Height. The top of the handrail gripping surface must be mounted between 34 and 38 inches (865 and 965 mm) above the stair nosing (ADAAG 4.9.4[5]).

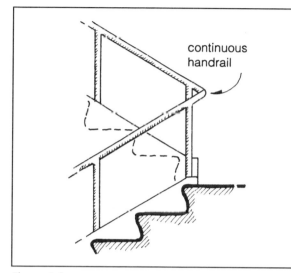

Figure 4-2

In schools, however, an additional handrail has been recommended at a height between 16 and 26 inches (406 and 660 mm) high, depending on the age of the children at a particular school (CAH 4.9.4). The proposed rule changes to ADAAG would require a second handrail mounted between 20 and 28 inches (510 and 710 mm) above stair nosings (ADAAG, Children's Facilities, 15.4.2).

Clearance. Clearance between the wall and the handrail or grab bar can have critical importance. Many people brace their forearms between supports and walls, giving themselves more leverage and stability when using ramps and stairs or when lifting their lower body during transfer activities at toilets

and showers. To prevent possible injury resulting from a person's arm slipping and becoming lodged between the wall and the bar, handrails must be located exactly 1-1/2 inches (38 mm) from any adjacent vertical surface (Figure 4-3) (ADAAG 4.9.4[3]). People may get their arms wedged in spaces that exceed this width. The wall surface behind the handrails must be smooth and free of sharp protrusions to prevent injury (ADAAG 4.26.4).

Recessed Handrails. If handrails are recessed into the wall, the recessed area must be no more than 3 inches (75 mm) deep and must extend at least 18 inches (455 mm) above the top of the handrail surface (Figure 4-3) (ADAAG 4.26.2).

Handrail Extensions. Handrails must extend at least 12 inches (305 mm) into the level area beyond a stairway's top riser and for a distance equal to one tread width plus 12 inches (305 mm) past the bottom riser (Figure 4-4). Extensions at the top of stairs must be parallel to the floor. Handrails at stair bottoms must continue to slope for one tread width beyond the bottom riser, with the remaining 12 inches (305 mm) extending horizontally (ADAAG 4.9.4[2]). Handrail extensions must not obstruct circulation paths.

Handrail Ends. The ends of handrails must be rounded or returned smoothly to a floor, wall, or post (ADAAG 4.9.4[6]). This design feature decreases the likelihood that people will catch their clothing or injure themselves on an exposed end.

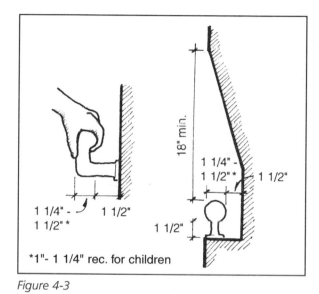

Figure 4-3

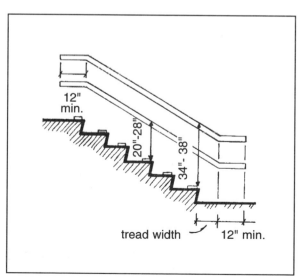

Figure 4-4

Detectable Warnings. Stair safety can be enhanced with the use of detectable warnings, which warn people of the presence of stairs. A variety of detectable warnings can be used, including visual cues, tactile cues, and variances in the sound or resilience of surface materials.

Visual Warnings. Some states have recognized that the visibility and safety of stairs are increased by using indicator stripping on stair treads. Designers should refer to state and local requirements for the size and placement of warning stripes at the edge of interior and exterior stair treads or the use of a sharply contrasting color to the tread surface at the front edge of nosings. Requirements for interior and exterior stairways may vary.

Tactile Warnings. Tactile warning strips extending the width of the stairway may be placed at the top and bottom landings to alert people to the presence of steps. To provide individuals with adequate time to adjust their gait, these warning strips should begin at least 36 inches (915 mm) before exterior stairs and extend to the top nosing (CAH 4.9.5).

Consistency. Consistent detectable warnings should be used throughout a school facility. Differently or haphazardly marked stairways can be confusing and dangerous for people who rely on these environmental cues.

Color Contrast. Handrails that contrast in color with surrounding materials provide cues for people with sight impairments. The use of contrasting colors helps people to locate the handrails and assess the extent of the ramp or stairs.

Wheelchair Lifts

Two major types of lifts are used for transporting individuals who are unable to negotiate stairs: the platform lift, which connects level changes of up to 12 feet (4.6 m), and the incline lift, which connects two or more floors.

Although lifts can increase accessibility, their use is subject to several limitations. In building alterations for accessibility upgrades to the path of travel, lifts should be restricted to providing access to areas where a change in level exists and a ramp or elevator cannot be used due to space or financial limitations (ADAAG 4.1.6[g]).

In new facilities, wheelchair lifts may only be used in place of an elevator in the following instances:

- To provide access to a performing area, such as the stage in an auditorium
- To provide accessible seating in different locations throughout an auditorium or tiered room (see Assembly Areas in Section V)
- To provide access to spaces and rooms that are not open to the public and have a maximum capacity of five people, such as equipment control rooms, projection booths, and stadium press boxes (the activities conducted in these areas usually require a location above the general viewing area and thus cannot take place elsewhere)
- To provide access to areas where site constraints do not allow the placement of an elevator or ramp (ADAAG 4.1.3 [Exception 4]).

The use of wheelchair lifts is not recommended for several reasons. For example, lifts in exterior locations are exposed to inclement weather and extreme temperatures, thus requiring more frequent maintenance than ramps or elevators. Lifts are noisy and draw attention to riders and their special needs. And, due to the limited space on most lift platforms, a person must ride alone, which can be a scary experience for young children. Many lifts require a key or a specially trained individual to operate them. Such lifts may not be accessible for events that take place outside regular school hours, such as afterschool and evening programs or community meetings and performances.

Security and safety issues must be closely examined when installing lifts. Administrators should be concerned about students playing around lifts and hurting themselves or damaging the lift. The load limit capabilities of the lift should be determined, and information regarding the various size and weight combinations of people and wheelchairs should be posted. Appropriate state and local codes should be consulted for specifications on the use of lifts, including the ASME A17.1 Safety Code for Elevators and Escalators.

Ramps

Ramps provide a method of negotiating vertical level changes without the use of stairs or mechanical lifting devices. Ramps are useful for wheelchair users as well as individuals with leg braces or hip pain. Ramps also assist people transporting items on dollies or carts. Designers should note, however, that some people who use walking aids or have low stamina often prefer stairs, because each tread provides a level surface for resting and realigning body posture (ADAAG A4.8.1).

Accessible ramps may be used instead of the elevators required to connect each level of a new multistory facility (ADAAG 4.1.3[5]).

Slope. Any part of an accessible route with a slope greater than 1:20 is considered a ramp and is subject to the following guidelines (ADAAG 4.8.1). Allowable slope requirements depend on the intended user and vary for new construction and building alterations. ADAAG requires that the least possible slope be used on any ramp (ADAAG 4.8.2).

The most restrictive requirements apply to new facilities and use by children. For instance, the slope of ramps intended for general use must not exceed 1:12 in new facilities (ADAAG 4.8.2), while those intended for children should not exceed 1:16

(CAH 4.8.2). However, to ensure complete access for all users, a sloping walk (with a ratio less than 1:20) is preferred whenever possible. In any case, ramps with slopes between 1:16 and 1:20 are preferred since they are more easily negotiated by most people who use wheelchairs, have low stamina, or possess poor upper-body strength (ADAAG 4.8.2, A4.8.2). The Access Board is currently conducting a research project on acceptable ramp slopes in children's environments. The results of this research will be incorporated into the new guidelines for children's facilities.

In renovated children's environments, if space limitations prohibit the construction of a ramp with a 1:16 slope or less, a ramp may have a slope of 1:12 for a maximum rise of 6 inches (150 mm). A slope steeper than 1:12 is difficult or impossible for most children to negotiate (CAH 4.8.2).

In renovated facilities that are not primarily intended for use by children, if space limitations prohibit the construction of a ramp with a slope of 1:12 or less, a ramp may have a slope between 1:10 and 1:12 for a maximum rise of 6 inches (150 mm) or a slope between 1:8 and 1:10 for a maximum rise of 3 inches (75 mm). A slope steeper than 1:8 is not allowed (ADAAG 4.1.6[3][a]).

Cross Slope. The cross slope of a ramp surface must not exceed 1:50 (ADAAG 4.8.6).

Rise. Although ADAAG currently limits ramps to a continuous rise of 30 inches (760 mm) or less (ADAAG 4.8.2), proposed rule changes to the allowable length of a ramp intended for children would further limit a continuous rise to 9-5/8 to 12 inches (245 to 305 mm).

Horizontal Run. The allowable length of a single run of ramp (i.e., horizontal distance) depends on the intended user and the slope of the ramp. For ramps used by children, the horizontal run for any slope should not exceed 20 feet (6 m) (CAH 4.8.2). For ramps not intended for use by children, if the slope is less than 1:16, a run must not exceed 40 feet (12 m) and, if the slope is steeper than 1:16, a run must not exceed 30 feet (9 m) (ADAAG 4.8.2).

Clear Width. Ramps must have a minimum clear width of 36 inches (915 mm) (ADAAG 4.8.3). For ramps used by children, the recommended minimum clear width is 44 inches (1120 mm). If the ramp is intended for two-way traffic by wheelchairs, the clear width should be 88 inches (2235 mm) to allow for passing room (CAH 4.8.3).

Landings. Ramps must have a level landing at the top and bottom of each run. Uneven landings may cause wheelchair users to tip backward or bottom out when approaching a ramp. Landings also provide rest areas and maneuvering space for changing direction. Landings must meet the following guidelines.

- Landings must be at least as wide as the ramp leading to them.
- Landings must measure at least 60 inches (1525 mm) long.
- If ramps change direction at a landing, the landing must measure at least 60 by 60 inches (1525 by 1525 mm).
- If a doorway is located at a landing, the maneuvering area in front of the doorway must be accessible to wheelchair users (ADAAG 4.8.4) (see Doors in this section).

When a turn into vehicular traffic is required at the bottom of ramps used by children, sufficient space must be provided for safe maneuvering. As a result, the turning space should be located beyond the required 60 inches (1524 mm) of clear landing (CAH 4.8.4).

Handrails. Handrails are required on both sides of ramp runs with a rise greater than 6 inches (150 mm) or a length (horizontal distance) exceeding 72 inches (1830 mm) (ADAAG 4.8.5). For ramps used by children, a second set of handrails placed below the standard handrails will enable children to use the ramp more easily and safely (ADAAG A4.8.5). Specifications for location, size, and shape of handrails for ramps are the same as for handrails on stairs.

Ramp Surfaces. Ramp surfaces must be stable, firm, and slip-resistant. Outdoor ramps must be designed to prevent the accumulation of water on their horizontal surfaces (ADAAG 4.8.8). The following tactics will help to ensure safe and usable ramp surfaces:

- Placing overhead coverings to screen the ramp surface
- Removing debris, leaves, sand, and snow regularly
- Installing subsurface heating coils to prevent the accumulation of ice.

Edge Protection. Ramps and landings with drop-offs must have barriers such as curbs, walls, or railings to prevent people from slipping off the edge. If curbs are installed, they must measure at least 2 inches (50 mm) high (ADAAG 4.8.7). The appropriate type of edge protection depends on the primary function of a ramp. Whereas delivery ramps may require curbs, ramps used by students may require walls or railings.

Doors

The design of accessible doors must take into account the weight and size of the door, the design of the threshold, the type of door hardware, and the maneuvering space in front of the door. When doors are not well-designed and strategically located, they may become barriers to accessibility.

Exterior doors must accommodate the movement of large groups of people during high traffic periods and must allow smooth evacuation of buildings in the event of an emergency. Interior doors separate one space from another and must provide privacy and quiet.

Location. In new facilities, accessible doors are required at the following locations:

- At least one door at each accessible entrance
- At least one door at each accessible room or space
- Each door that is part of the accessible route
- Each door that is required to be accessible for purposes of egress (ADAAG 4.1.3[7]).

Clear Width. Doors must have a minimum clear width of 32 inches (815 mm) with the door open 90 degrees (Figure 4-5). This distance is measured between the face of the door and the opposite door stop. If the depth of the doorway exceeds 24 inches (610 mm), however, then the clear width must measure at least 36 inches (915 mm) (ADAAG 4.13.5).

Doors that do not require users to pass completely through them, such as doors to shallow closets, require a reduced minimum clear width of 20 inches (510 mm) (ADAAG 4.13.5).

Maneuvering Space. For a door to be considered accessible, a person using a wheelchair or other mobility aid must be able to approach the door, operate the opening mechanism, and have enough maneuvering space to swing the door open and pass through. The amount of space needed depends on the type of door, the manner in which it must be approached (such as after a 90-degree turn from a narrow hallway, or after a forward approach from a level deck), and whether the approach is from the latch or hinge side. In all instances, maneuvering clearance areas should be level and free of obstructions (Figures 4-6, 4-7, and 4-8) (ADAAG 4.13.6). Maneuvering clearance areas for sliding doors are illustrated in Figures 4-9, 4-10, and 4-11.

Opening Force. Door weight and opening force are critical issues for people with low stamina, mobility limitations, or upper-extremity weakness. For instance, fire doors must be heavy and securely shut to fulfill their function, yet all individuals must be able to open these doors to reach areas of rescue assistance. Therefore, fire doors must have the minimum opening force allowed by the appropriate administrative authority.

The maximum force for pushing or pulling open a door used by children should not exceed 5 lbf (22.2 N) (CAH 4.13.11). Local ordinances provide minimum force requirements for pushing or pulling open exterior doors used primarily by adults. The maximum force to open sliding doors, folding doors,

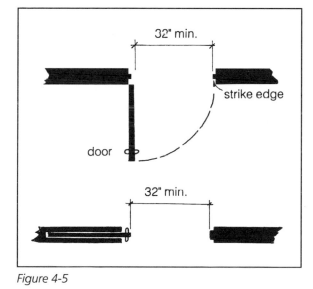

Figure 4-5

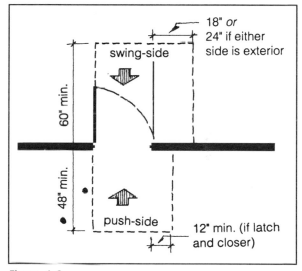

Figure 4-6

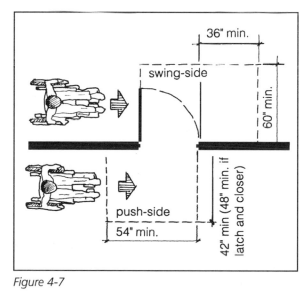

Figure 4-7

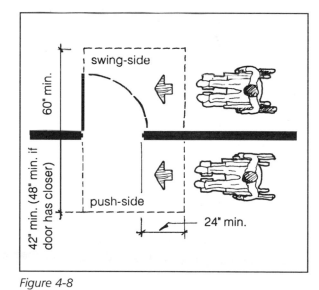

Figure 4-8

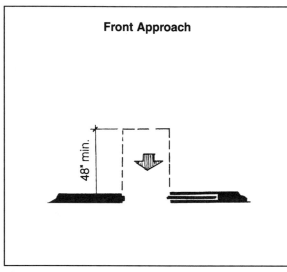

Figure 4-9

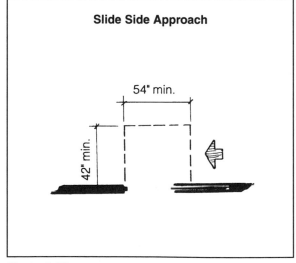

Figure 4-10

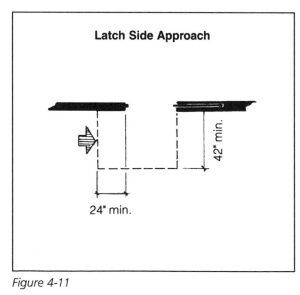

Figure 4-11

or interior hinged doors is required to be 5 lbf (22.2 N) or less (ADAAG 4.13.11).

Threshold Height. Most wheelchair users find it difficult or impossible to maneuver a wheelchair up and over a threshold that exceeds 1/2 inch (13 mm) in height. This task is further complicated if the users must manipulate a door handle while pushing open a door. Raised thresholds also pose tripping hazards.

All thresholds used by children should not exceed 1/2 inch (13 mm) (CAH 4.13.8). Thresholds must not exceed 3/4 inch (19 mm) in height for exte-

rior sliding doors or 1/2 inch (13 mm) for all other types of doors used primarily by adults.

Raised thresholds at accessible doorways must be beveled with a slope that does not exceed 1:2 (ADAAG 4.13.8).

In renovated facilities, existing thresholds may measure up to 3/4 inch (19 mm) in height, so long as they have beveled edges on each side (ADAAG 4.1.6[d][ii]).

Door Hardware. Operating devices on accessible doors—such as handles, pulls, latches, and locks—must be easy to grasp with one hand and must not require tight grasping, pinching, or twisting of the wrist to operate. Acceptable designs include lever handles, push-type mechanisms (for example, panic bars), and U-shaped handles, all of which are easier for children to operate. These devices also accommodate the needs of people with a weak grasp, poor hand coordination, or painful joints (ADAAG 4.13.9).

Hardware on accessible doors must be within easy reach of all users. Hardware on doors used by children should be mounted no higher than 30 to 34 inches (760 to 865 mm) above the floor; however, panic bars may be mounted 30 to 36 inches (760 to 915 mm) above the floor (CAH 4.13.9), but they must not protrude more than 4 inches (100 mm) into the door opening when the door is fully open. For doors used primarily by adults, hardware must be mounted no higher than 48 inches (1220 mm) above the floor (ADAAG 4.13.9).

According to conventional design practices, most door hardware is mounted 36 inches (915 mm) from the floor. The Access Board is currently investigating if this height is appropriate for use by children as well as if hardware mounted at lower heights is usable by adults. The result of its inquiry will determine future rule changes to ADAAG, since most doors must be operable by children and adults alike.

Operating hardware on sliding doors must be exposed and usable from both sides when these doors are fully opened (ADAAG 4.13.9).

Closers. Closers automatically shut doors after they have been opened, a useful feature for reducing noise, maintaining privacy, and reducing stress on heating and cooling systems. Closers also free people from having to shut the door behind them, which is a difficult task for some individuals.

When closers are used, they must be adjusted so that a slow-moving person has sufficient time to pass through the threshold without getting hit by the door. The door must take at least 3 seconds to travel from an open position of 70 degrees to a point 3 inches (75 mm) from the latch (ADAAG 4.13.10).

Auxiliary Handle. For doors that do not have a closer but need to be closed for privacy, such as doors to bathroom stalls or private study areas, an auxiliary handle may be added near the hinge side of the door. These handles allow people using mobility aids to pull the door closed as they pass through the threshold. Auxiliary handles should be positioned vertically and located at heights appropriate for the intended user.

Kickplates. People using wheelchairs, walkers, canes, or crutches frequently use their mobility aid to push open a door or to hold the door open as they pass through the threshold.

To reduce potential damage caused by these actions, kickplates may be attached along the bottom of doors. Kickplates should span the width of the door, less 1 inch (25 mm) on each side, and should extend upward at least 16 inches (405 mm) from the bottom edge of the door (ADAAG A4.13.9).

Vision Panel. Door vision panels provide windows to check that the swing area is clear before opening the door. They should be located on the latch side of the door and measure at least 3 inches (75 mm) wide. The bottom of vision panels should be located no more than 36 inches (915 mm) from the floor to ensure that younger students can use them.

Automatic Doors

At times, automatic doors provide the best solution for achieving accessibility. Since they require no or little force to operate, they are especially beneficial to people who use mobility aids, possess limited strength or stamina, or are carrying items. They also may eliminate the need for extra maneuvering space and help to keep traffic flowing at an even pace.

Automatic doors should be considered in the following circumstances:

- When existing doors are too heavy
- When doors are located in heavily used public areas
- When 18 inches (455 mm) of clear space is not available on the latch side of the door or where there is insufficient maneuvering space in front of the door.

Automatic doors must comply with ANSI/BHMA A156.10-1985, and slowly opening, low-powered automatic doors must comply with ANSI A156.19-1984 (ADAAG 4.13.12).

Types of Automatic Doors. Sliding automatic doors are generally preferred to hinged versions, particularly in areas with heavy two-way pedestrian traffic. Since hinged automatic doors require ample clear floor space to accommodate the swing of the door, they may create a hazard for people with visual limitations who unknowingly enter the swinging door's path.

Operation. Automatic doors can be activated by a pressure-sensitive mat, a pendant switch, a foot-

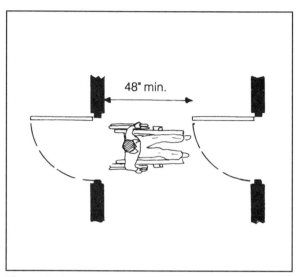

Figure 4-12

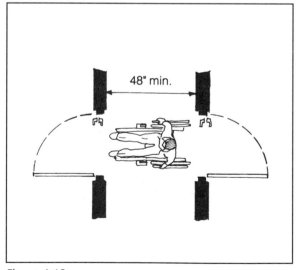

Figure 4-13

or hand-operated push-button, or a photo-cell sensing device. Activation switches or buttons should be located along the path of travel, clearly visible, and mounted on a side wall or post at a height within easy reach of all users (see Door Hardware above). When they are mounted on a post, the post must not reduce the minimum clear width of a pathway (see Protruding Objects in Section II).

Timing. Automatic door closers should be adjusted to allow sufficient time for slow-moving individuals to cross the threshold.

To minimize hazards, automatic doors also must take at least 3 seconds to open and must not require more than 15 lbf (66.6 N) to stop movement (ADAAG 4.13.12).

Alternate Route. In areas where automatic doors are used, a non-automatic, side-hung door should be available nearby in case of power failure when people are not able to open the automatic doors manually.

Doors: Special Situations

Double-Leaf Doorways. School entrances often have double-leaf doorways, which increase efficiency and safety at peak periods of use. If each door in a double-leaf doorway operates independently, at least one door must be fully accessible, although it is recommended that both provide full access (ADAAG 4.13.4).

An 18-inch (455 mm) panel to separate the doors in a double-leaf doorway provides the required maneuvering space on the latch side of each door and keeps people from being struck if the other door is opened.

Doors in Sequence. Doors in sequence are often used at entrances to shield building interiors from extreme outdoor temperatures and in the interior to provide added privacy at restroom entrances. The distance between two doors in sequence must measure at least 48 inches (1220 mm) in addition to the width of any door swinging into this area in order to provide sufficient maneuvering space for people using mobility aids. The doors must swing either in the same direction or away from the area between the doors (Figures 4-12 and 4-13) (ADAAG 4.13.7).

Glass Doors. Glass doors should be made of impact-resistant material such as fiberglass, tempered glass, or polycarbonate glass. Visual cues, such as horizontal bars placed at eye level, will signal the presence of glass to people with low visual ability. In addition, a kickplate should be attached to the bottom of a glass door to enable people using mobility aids to push open the door safely.

Revolving Doors and Turnstiles. Revolving doors and turnstiles should be avoided whenever possible because they are difficult or impossible to use by people with mobility limitations. If their use cannot be avoided, an adjacent, accessible gate or door that permits the same pattern of travel must be provided (ADAAG 4.13.2).

Elevators

ADAAG provides specific guidelines for elevators. Elevators should comply with these standards, in addition to the associated reach range and clear floor space requirements discussed earlier.

Moving through the Building

Orientation and Wayfinding

The design and layout of a school can directly affect the ability of users to negotiate their way through the facility. A well-designed environment facilitates the two activities most needed for successful navigation: orientation and wayfinding. Orientation refers to the process of locating oneself in an environment relative to place, time, and people. Wayfinding refers to the process of systematically proceeding from an initial point to a final destination.

People rely on cognitive maps to provide structured, mental images of an environment. For example, a student's cognitive map of her school might focus on particular rooms and their relation to each other, such as the image of the cafeteria and gymnasium sitting at opposite ends of the site with the library located directly in the middle. This map might also include the general location of other rooms situated between each key reference point. By using this mental map, the student can orient herself and navigate her way through the environment, without knowing the exact identity and location of most rooms. To assist children in developing cognitive maps, designers should create schools arranged in a clear, logical manner with structural elements that can serve as appropriate landmarks.

Orientation and wayfinding require the use of visual, proprioceptive, and tactile senses, as well as motor and cognitive abilities. Navigation skills are developed through early childhood motor and tactile experiences. Children with disabilities may have had fewer experiences and may need additional assistance in establishing effective orientation and wayfinding skills.

The application of the following strategies will help to facilitate orientation and wayfinding in school settings.

Circulation Design.   Orientation and wayfinding become more difficult as choices increase among different paths of travel. Simple, logical, and consistent layouts are easier to remember. Routes should be direct and linear rather than intersecting or branching. Changes in direction should be delineated explicitly; for example, 90-degree turns are more memorable than slight turns.

Landmarks.   The placement of prominent design elements in corridors, wings, and major junctions will assist individuals in wayfinding. Such landmarks should be obvious, distinct, and permanent. Landmarks for children should consist of tangible objects (such as a telephone booth) rather than abstract symbols.

Use of Contrasting Colors.   Wayfinding can be enhanced by using contrasting colors—light against dark, bright against dull—to highlight perimeters and boundary edges. The color of the floor, for example, could contrast with the color of the wall. However, the use of color contrasting or coding should not be used as the sole means of identifying different parts of a school facility.

Place Names.   Providing names for different buildings, corridors, and other spaces in a facility will assist individuals in creating cognitive maps of the environment.

Minimized Distractions.   Visual distractions and noise can hamper wayfinding for some people with disabilities. Complicated floor and wall patterns should be avoided. Background noise should be minimized (see Lighting, HVAC, and Acoustics in Section V).

Obstructions. Circulation routes must be free from objects that can become accessibility barriers for people using mobility aids or hazards for people with visual limitations (see Protruding Objects in Section II).

Signage

Well-designed, consistently placed signs throughout a school facility can provide valuable assistance in orientation and wayfinding by providing comprehensive directions and information. Signs are particularly important in such potentially confusing environments as stairwells and places where the accessible route differs from the primary route of travel. Directional signs should be provided periodically to assure individuals that they are on the correct path.

Signs in school facilities serve three specific functions: identifying permanent rooms and spaces, providing directions, and displaying information. Since these signs must communicate to children as well as adults, they must be designed carefully to reach the widest range of users.

Signs should be clear and explicit. The use of simple words and pictograms will aid comprehension by young children, non-native speakers, and people with cognitive limitations. Signs should be consistent in wall placement, mounting height, color, typeface, and terminology throughout the school.

Special Signs for Accessible Features. The following accessible features must be identified by signs bearing the International Symbol of Accessibility:

- Parking spaces designated for individuals with disabilities
- Accessible passenger loading zones
- Accessible entrances when not all are accessible (non-accessible entrances must indicate the route to the nearest accessible entrance)
- Accessible toilet and bathing facilities when not all are accessible (ADAAG 4.1.2[7]).

Location. Informational, directional, or identifying signs are recommended at the following locations:

- Building entrances (building directory)
- Accessible routes (directional signs)
- Classrooms, offices, and common areas (identification signs)
- Stairwells and ramps (floor identification signs, directional signs)
- Elevators (floor identification signs, directional signs)
- Telephones (identification signs, assistive listening device signs)

- Permanent or temporary hazards (warning signs)
- Restrooms (identification signs, International Symbol of Accessibility).

Signs for Permanent Spaces. Identifying signs for permanent spaces (for example, room number signs) must be mounted on the wall adjacent to the latch side of the door. When wall space is not available, signs must be placed on the nearest adjacent wall. Although the Access Board has not yet determined the appropriate height for signs intended for use by children, tactile signs should be mounted at a lower height than is required for those used by adults—with the centerline measuring 48 inches (1220 mm) from the floor according to CAH 4.30.6 or 42 inches according to other sources. Signs intended for adult use only must measure 60 inches (1525 mm) from the floor (Figure 4-14) (ADAAG 4.30.6).

To permit close reading or touch-reading, people must be able to approach within 3 inches (75 mm) of the sign without entering the swing area of a door (ADAAG 4.30.6). Sufficient clear floor space also must be provided to enable people using mobility aids to approach the signs (see Clear Floor Space in Section II).

Sign surfaces must have an eggshell, matte, or other non-glare finish. Characters on signs must contrast in color with the background to ensure visibility and legibility (ADAAG 4.30.5).

Characters must be raised 1/32 inches (0.79 mm) and measure between 5/8 and 2 inches (16 and 50 mm) high. Letters must be upper case and set in a sans serif or simple serif typeface. Raised characters must be accompanied with Grade 2 Braille (ADAAG 4.30.4). Signs with pictograms must include a written version of the message directly below the symbol. The pictogram must measure at least 6 inches (150 mm) high (ADAAG 4.30.4).

Directional and Informational Signs.   Signs that provide directions or other types of information (except building directories and temporary signs) must meet the following guidelines (ADAAG 4.1.3[16]).

Sign surfaces must have an eggshell, matte, or other non-glare finish. Characters on signs must contrast in color with the background to ensure visibility and legibility (ADAAG 4.30.5).

Letters and numbers must follow standard proportions (Figure 4-15). The ratio of character width to character height must measure between 3:5 and 1:1. The ratio of line width to letter height must measure between 1:5 and 1:10 (ADAAG 4.30.2).

Overhead Signs.   Since people with limited vision may have difficulty in reading overhead signs, upper-case letters and numbers used on them must measure at least 3 inches (75 mm) in height (ADAAG 4.30.3). People with limited or no vision might not even be able to detect the presence of overhead signs. To provide a sufficiently safe head clearance for adults at school facilities, the bottom edge of overhead signs must hang at least 80 inches (2030 mm) above the floor (ADAAG 4.4.2).

Assistive Listening Device Signs.   The availability and location of technological adaptations for hearing loss, such as volume control and text telephones, must be identified by signs (see Telephones in this section).

Emergency Systems

School facilities must meet emergency system guidelines, including those for emergency warning devices, evacuation routes, and rescue assistance areas. This section discusses only those issues addressed by the ADA guidelines and advocates of universal design. Designers and facility managers must consult local authorities for specific life-safety codes.

Alarms

Alarms often provide the first warning of an emergency. To be effective, alarms must provide their signal in an understandable form and in a timely manner throughout a facility. As a result, emergency warning systems must incorporate both visual and audible alarms (ADAAG 4.1.3[14]). To

Figure 4-14

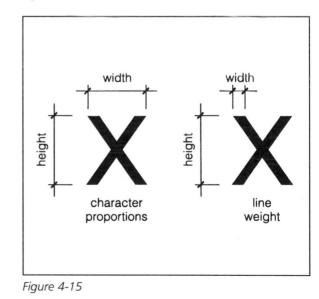

Figure 4-15

prevent confusion, the particular pulse and pitch of alarms should be exclusive to and different from sounds signaling public announcements or classroom bells.

Audible Alarms. To ensure that individuals with hearing limitations are alerted to emergencies, audible alarms must produce a sound that either exceeds the prevailing sound level in the area by at least 15 dbA or exceeds any maximum sound level of one-minute duration by 5 dbA, whichever sound is louder. However, the sound level of audible alarms must not exceed 120 dbA (ADAAG 4.28.2). Alarms with periodic pauses or changes in their signal, such as single-stroke bells and hi-low signals, are recommended because of their greater ability to attract people's attention (ADAAG A4.28.2). Designers should note that the prevailing noise level will vary in different parts of a facility, depending on the size and function of the space. For example, the noise level in the school gymnasium usually exceeds the noise level in the staff lounge.

Visual Alarms. At a minimum, visual alarms such as flashing lights must be provided in school restrooms, hallways, lobbies, and other common use areas (ADAAG 4.28.1). Visual alarms must be integrated into the facility alarm system. If single-station audible alarms are provided (as opposed to a facility-wide alarm system), then single-station

visual alarm signals must also be provided (ADAAG 4.28.3). Visual alarms must also meet the following guidelines.

- The signal must consist of a xenon strobe light or equivalent.
- The signal must consist of unfiltered or clear filtered white light.
- The pulse duration (the interval between the initial and final points of 10 percent of the maximum signal) must not last more than 0.2 seconds with a maximum duty cycle of 40 percent.
- The flash rate must fall between 1 and 3 Hz
- The alarm must be placed either 80 inches (2030 mm) above the floor or 6 inches (152 mm) below the ceiling, whichever height is lower.
- The visual signal must not be more than 50 feet (15 m) from any part of a room or space required to have visual alarms (measured horizontally). However, in spaces that exceed 100 feet (30 m) in width and are free of obstructions 6 feet (2 m) above the floor, visual alarms may be placed around the perimeter of the room at a maximum interval of 100 feet (30 m) (ADAAG 4.28.3).

Additional Alarms. Visual alarms should also be installed in any private work areas of a school used by students or employees with hearing limitations. Work areas can be adapted by installing a strobe light, vibrator, or fan as part of the emergency system.

Hazard Warnings. Although the ADA guidelines do not cover hazard warnings, designers and managers should ensure that hazards such as construction scaffolding are marked with sufficient warnings. Appropriate warnings include signs and detectable changes in the walking surface.

Fire Pull Stations. Fire pull stations should not require more than 8 lbf (35.5 N) to operate. The operating control of a pull station should be located between 24 and 48 inches (610 and 1220 mm) above the floor. In order for fire pull controls to be accessible to children, they should be placed between 20 and 36 inches (510 and 915 mm) above the floor, and they should require no more than 5 lbf (22.2 N) to operate (CAH 4.2.5–6).

Portable Telephones and Beepers. Students who are not independently mobile should receive a portable telephone or beeper for use on the school grounds. These devices enable such students to call for assistance if they get into a hazardous situation.

Emergency Call Switches. Emergency call switches, which activate an alarm to call for help, should be located in restrooms. The device can consist of a pull cord or push bar located no more than 48 inches (1220 mm) above the floor for adults and between 20 and 36 inches (510 and 915 mm) above the floor for children. This system should also include a method of two-way communication or a means to signal that the call for help has been received.

Egress Requirements and Areas of Rescue Assistance

To enhance the sense of security and well-being for all members of the school community, emergency egress routes and areas of rescue assistance must be accessible and clearly marked. Areas of rescue assistance are places in a building where people with disabilities can wait in safety for help during emergency evacuations. These areas are not required in facilities with automatic fire sprinkler systems (ADAAG 4.1.3[9]). People who may use an area of rescue assistance during an emergency should receive instruction on the specific procedures to be followed.

Evacuation Procedures. All accessible routes must lead to an accessible outdoor area or an accessible area of rescue assistance (ADAAG 4.3.10). School administrators must develop and practice emergency evacuation procedures for individuals with disabilities, including visitors. Preparations must be reviewed routinely to account for the needs of new students or staff (ADAAG A4.3.10).

Location. Areas of rescue assistance must be located in one of the following places:

- A stairway landing within a smoke-proof enclosure
- A section of an exterior exit balcony adjacent to an exit stairway (exits from the building must be located within 20 feet [6 m] of the area and must have a 45-minute fire protection rating)
- A portion of a stairway landing within an exit enclosure
- A room or area that is separated from other parts of the building by a smoke barrier
- A section of a corridor or vestibule with a one-hour fire protection rating that is located adjacent to an exit enclosure (stairwell)
- An elevator lobby where the shaft(s) and lobby are pressurized by equipment activated by smoke detectors (this equipment and required duct work must have a two-hour fire protection rating) *or*
- An area approved by the appropriate local authority (ADAAG 4.3.11.1).

Size. Each area of rescue assistance must provide a minimum of two wheelchair spaces, each measuring at least 30 by 48 inches (760 by 122 mm). At least one wheelchair space must be provided on each floor; additional wheelchair spaces must be provided at a ratio of one for every 200 occupants of that floor. If floor occupancy totals less than 200, the appropriate local authority may reduce the required number of wheelchair spaces per area of rescue assistance to one (ADAAG 4.3.11.2).

Stairway Width. The clear width between handrails of a stairway adjacent to an area of rescue assistance must measure at least 48 inches (1220 mm) (ADAAG 4.3.11.3). This width provides enough space for two people to carry an individual down the stairs.

Two-Way Communication. To ensure that people do not get stranded in an area of rescue assistance, means for two-way communication between the area and the primary entrance must be provided. The device must include both audible and visible signals to ensure that people with hearing, speech, and visual limitations can communicate. If the primary entrance is not an appropriate receiving station, the fire department or other local authority may approve an alternate location for the other end of the two-way communication (ADAAG 4.3.11.4).

Signage. Areas of rescue assistance must be identified with a sign bearing the words "Area of Rescue Assistance" and displaying the International Symbol of Accessibility. This sign must be illuminated when local codes require the illumination of exit signs (ADAAG 4.3.11.5).

A sign next to the two-way communication system must provide clear instructions on its use during emergencies. Additional signs must be installed at non-accessible exits and along paths of travel to

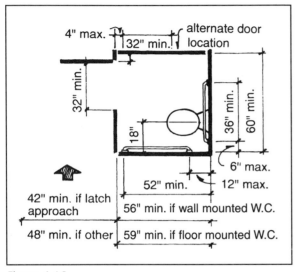

Figure 4-16

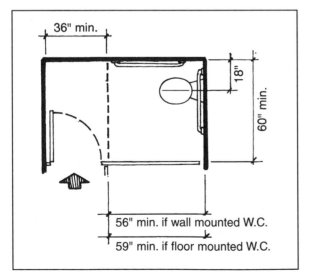

Figure 4-17

indicate the most direct route to areas of rescue assistance (ADAAG 4.3.11.5).

Restrooms

School restrooms, referred to as "toilet rooms" in the ADA guidelines, must be designed to provide the greatest possible degree of privacy and independence for all users. Many wheelchair users can relate embarrassing experiences about attempts to use a non-accessible restroom. Restroom accessibility ranks second only to general building accessibility, according to U.S. Department of Justice guidelines that set priorities for ADA renovations. Designers should note that standards for new construction can differ from those for renovation projects.

Toilet rooms may be configured to serve either one user at a time or multiple users. All new public and common-use toilet rooms must be accessible and located along an accessible route (ADAAG 4.1.3[11], 4.22.1).

Doors. All doors to accessible toilet rooms must comply with ADA guidelines (see Doors under Entering and Exiting the Building). Doors must not swing into the required clear floor space for any fixture (ADAAG 4.22.2).

Clear Floor Space. To ensure accessibility, appropriate clear floor space must be provided at each accessible fixture (see Clear Floor Space in Section II). Unobstructed turning space for wheelchair users must also be provided within the toilet room; this space must measure at least 60 inches (1525 mm) in diameter. Areas of clear floor space may overlap (ADAAG 4.22.3).

Toilet Stalls

All accessible toilet stalls must be located along an accessible route and contain a water closet (i.e., toilet) that complies with ADA guidelines (ADAAG 4.17.1–2).

Size and Arrangement of Stalls. If the toilet room contains stalls, at least one stall must comply with guidelines for the standard accessible stall, illustrated in Figure 4-16 (ADAAG 4.17.3).

The stall depth must be at least 59 inches (1500 mm) if the water closet is floor-mounted; it may be reduced to 56 inches (1420 mm) if the water closet is wall-mounted. The centerline of the water closet must measure 18 inches (455 mm) from one side wall or partition. The layout shown may be reversed to allow either a left- or right-hand approach. Figure 4-17 illustrates a standard stall at the end of a row.

Proposed rule changes for children's facilities would require standard accessible stalls to have a minimum depth of 59 inches (1500 mm) whether a floor- and wall-mounted water closet is used.

Standard stalls at the end of a row would be required to have a minimum 59-inch (1500 mm) depth in addition to the minimum 36 inches (915 mm) for the stall door (ADAAG, Children's Facilities, 15.7.3).

Additional proposed rule changes would shorten the required distance between the water closet centerline and one side wall or partition (Table 4-1) (ADAAG, Children's Facilities, 15.6.2). These centerline requirements would not apply to the 36-inch (915 mm) wide alternate stall described below.

ADA guidelines require the use of the standard accessible stall in new construction. The standard stall must also be used in restroom renovations, unless it is not feasible due to excessive cost, space constraints, or local plumbing codes—in which case, either of the alternate stall designs illustrated in Figures 4-18 and 4-19 may be substituted (ADAAG A4.17.3).

If the toilet room contains six or more stalls, then at least one stall, in addition to the standard stall, must comply with guidelines for the 36-inch (915 mm) wide alternate design (ADAAG 4.17.3). The 36-inch (915 mm) wide alternate design is not recommended for use in children's environments because small children may not be able to reach and get a secure hold on the grab bars (CAH 4.17.3).

In both alternate designs, the stall depth must be at least 69 inches (1745 mm) if the water closet is floor-mounted; it may be reduced to 66 inches (1675

TABLE 4-1 SPECIFICATIONS FOR WATER CLOSETS

AGES	WATER CLOSET CENTERLINE (MEASURED FROM ONE SIDE WALL OR PARTITION)
2 through 4	12 inches (305 mm)
5 through 8	12 to 15 inches (305 to 380 mm)
9 through 12	15 to 18 inches (380 to 455 mm)

mm) if the water closet is wall-mounted. Proposed rule changes for children's facilities, however, would require alternate accessible stalls to have a minimum depth of 69 inches (1745 mm) whether a floor- or wall-mounted water closet is used (ADAAG, Children's Facilities, 15.7.3).

The standard stall and the 48-inch (1220 mm) wide alternate design are usable by children of all ages.

Toe Clearance. Toe clearance in a toilet stall refers to the open space between the floor and the bottom edge of the stall partition. This clearance provides space for wheelchair footrests and increases the amount of maneuvering space within the stall.

For toilet stalls intended for use by children, the front partition and at least one side partition should provide a minimum toe clearance of 12 inches (305 mm) above the floor. This clearance is not required if the depth of the stall is greater than 60 inches

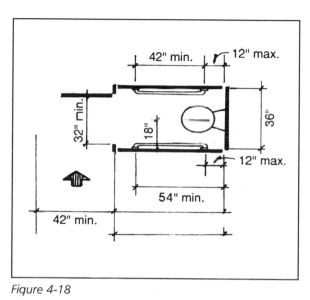

Figure 4-18

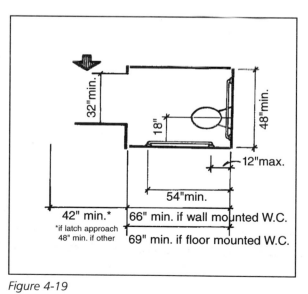

Figure 4-19

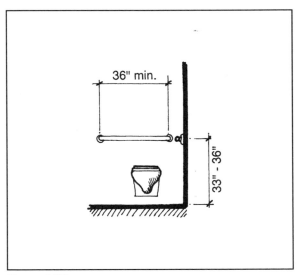

Figure 4-20

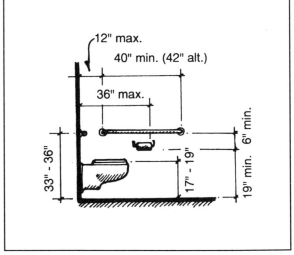

Figure 4-21

(1525 mm) (CAH 4.17.4 and ADAAG, Children's Facilities, 15.7.4).

For toilet stalls intended for use by adults, the front partition and at least one side partition must provide a minimum toe clearance of 9 inches (230 mm) above the floor. This clearance is not required if the depth of the stall is greater than 60 inches (1525 mm) (ADAAG 4.17.4).

Stall Doors. A door to an accessible toilet stall, including its operating hardware, must comply with ADA guidelines (ADAAG 4.17.5) (see Doors under Entering and Exiting the Building). Once inside a toilet stall, a person using a wheelchair or other mobility aid may find it difficult to close an outwardly swinging door. The addition of closers, spring hinges, or auxiliary handles on the insides of doors may help with this process (ADAAG A4.17.5).

The clearance between a closed stall door and any obstruction (for instance, a wall) must measure at least 48 inches (1220 mm). This clearance allows a person to reach the latch, open the door, maneuver around the door, and go into the stall. This clearance may be reduced to 42 inches (1065 mm) if the latch side of the stall door is nearest to a person approaching the stall, since the person will not need to maneuver around the door to enter the stall (ADAAG 4.17.5).

Size and Spacing of Grab Bars. The diameter or width of the gripping surface of a grab bar intended for use by children should be 1 to 1-1/4 inches (25 to 32 mm) (ADAAG, Children's Facilities, 15.6.3). The diameter or width of the gripping surface of a grab bar intended for use by adults must be 1-1/4 to 1-1/2 inches (32 to 38 mm). If grab bars are mounted adjacent to a wall, the space between the wall and the grab bar must be exactly 1-1/2 inches (38 mm) (ADAAG 4.26.2).

The required length and positioning of grab bars are illustrated in Figures 4-16, 4-18, 4-19, 4-20, and 4-21. Grab bars may be mounted with any desired method as long as they have a gripping surface at the locations shown and do not obstruct the required clear floor area (ADAAG 4.17.6).

Grab Bar Height. Grab bars should be mounted parallel to the floor. Designers should refer to state and local regulations regarding grab bar heights, which may be more restrictive than the following specifications.

For adults, the top of any grab bar used for water closets must measure between 33 and 36 inches (840 and 915 mm) above the floor (ADAAG 4.16.4).

Proposed rule changes for grab bars intended for use by children supplement earlier CAH recommendations (CAH 4.16.4a). The following table is based on specifications found in ADAAG, Children's Facilities, 15.6.2.

TABLE 4-2 SPECIFICATIONS FOR GRAB BARS

AGES	GRAB BAR HEIGHT
2 through 4	18 to 20 inches (455 to 510 mm)
5 through 8	20 to 25 inches (510 to 635 mm)
9 through 12	25 to 27 inches (635 to 685 mm)

In addition, rear grab bars intended for use by children should be placed at the lowest possible height that allows comfortable use without interference from the toilet tank or flush valve (CAII 4.16.4a).

Structural Strength of Grab Bars. All grab bars must support 250 lbf (1112 N) and must not rotate in their fittings (ADAAG 4.26.3). Refer to ADAAG 4.26.3 for specific guidelines on the structural strength of grab bars.

Hazards. Grab bars and adjacent walls must not have sharp edges or abrasive surfaces. Grab bar edges must be rounded, with a minimum radius of 1/8 inch (3.2 mm) (ADAAG 4.26.4).

Water Closets

All water closets (i.e., toilets) in accessible stalls, and at least one water closet if no stalls are provided, must comply with ADA guidelines (ADAAG 4.17.2, 4.22.4, and 4.23.4).

Clear Floor Space. Sufficient clear floor space in front of or beside a water closet is essential for people using mobility aids. Figure 4-22 outlines clear floor space requirements for water closets not located in stalls. This clear floor space can be arranged to accommodate either a left- or right-side transfer (ADAAG 4.16.2). Wheelchair users use this clear space to position their chairs near the water closet and safely transfer onto the toilet seat. Due to individual strengths and preferences, not all people use the same transfer methods, so the arrangement of the clear space should allow for as much flexibility as possible. In some cases, an individual may require the assistance of one or more people or the use of a mechanical lift to transfer onto a water closet.

Seat Height. For adults, the height of an accessible water closet must be between 17 and 19 inches (430 and 485 mm) (ADAAG 4.16.3). All seat heights for water closets are measured to the top of the seat.

The proposed rule changes for water closets intended for use by children supplement earlier CAH recommendations (CAH 4.16.3). The following table is based on specifications found in ADAAG, Children's Facilities, 15.6.2.

When deciding which seat height is appropriate for use in a particular toilet room, the ages of potential users should be considered. Thus, accessible

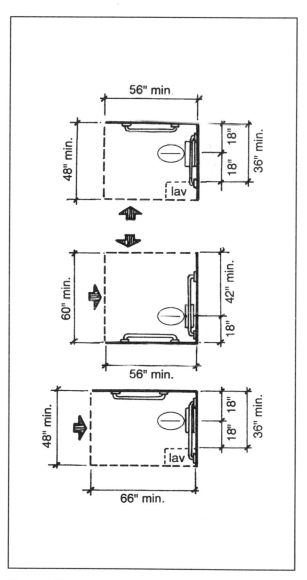

Figure 4-22

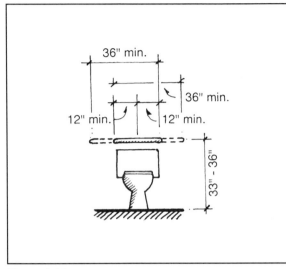

Figure 4-23

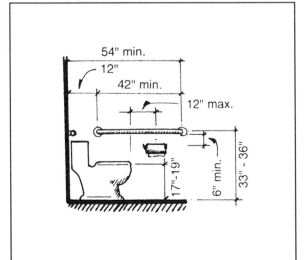

Figure 4-24

TABLE 4-3 SPECIFICATIONS FOR TOILET SEATS	
AGES	**TOILET SEAT HEIGHT**
2 through 4	11 to 12 inches (280 to 305 mm)
5 through 8	12 to 15 inches (305 to 380 mm)
9 through 12	15 to 17 inches (380 to 430 mm)

water closets in toilet rooms used solely by children should all have lowered heights, whereas toilet rooms used by adults and children (for example, those located near the school auditorium) should provide water closets with varying seat heights.

Spring Seat Hinges. Spring hinges must not be used to keep the toilet seat in a raised position when not in use (ADAAG 4.16.3). Because the spring action requires a person to push and hold the seat down, the hinges create an additional encumbrance for people with disabilities when transferring onto the seat.

Grab Bars. Grab bars for water closets not located in stalls must comply with the requirements outlined under Toilet Stalls and in Figures 4-23 and 4-24.

Flush Controls. Flush controls must be automatic or operable with one hand. Their operation must not require more than 5 lbf (22.2 N), or tight grasping, pinching, or twisting of the wrist (ADAAG 4.27.4). Flush controls must be mounted on the wide side of toilet areas.

For children, flush controls should be positioned within the reach ranges specified in Table 2-1 (see Reach Ranges in Section II) (ADAAG, Children's Facilities, 15.6.4).

For adults, flush controls must be positioned no more than 44 inches (1220 mm) above the floor (ADAAG 4.16.5).

Dispensers. Toilet paper dispensers must permit a continuous sheet of paper to be obtained without pinching, grasping, or twisting of the wrist. Dispensers must be installed within the reach of the water closet, as shown in Figure 4-24, and must be at least 6 inches (150 mm) below the grab bar so as not to interfere with its use (ADAAG 4.16.6).

Toilet paper dispensers intended for use by adults must be installed at least 19 inches (485 mm) above the floor (ADAAG 4.16.6).

Proposed rule changes for toilet paper dispensers intended for use by children supplement earlier CAH recommendations (CAH 4.16.6). The following table is based on specifications found in ADAAG, Children's Facilities, 15.6.2.

TABLE 4-4 SPECIFICATIONS FOR TOILET PAPER DISPENSERS	
AGES	**DISPENSER HEIGHT**
2 through 4	14 inches (355 mm)
5 through 8	14 to 17 inches (355 to 430 mm)
9 through 12	17 to 19 inches (430 to 485 mm)

Urinals

If urinals are provided, at least one must comply with the following (ADAAG 4.22.5 and 4.23.5).

Height. Accessible urinals must be stall-type or hung from the wall with an elongated rim (ADAAG 4.18.2).

Urinals used by children should be positioned so that the rim is no higher than 14 inches (356 mm) above the floor (CAH 4.18.2). Urinals used by adults must be positioned so that the rim is no higher than 17 inches (430 mm) above the floor (ADAAG 4.18.2). These heights allow use from a standing position and a comfortable reach for emptying catheter leg bags from a seated position.

Clear Floor Space. While clear floor space in front of urinals intended for use by adults must measure at least 30 by 48 inches (760 by 1220 mm)

(ADAAG 4.18.3), proposed rule changes for urinals intended for use by children would increase the requirements to 36 by 48 inches (915 by 1220 mm). This clear space must adjoin or overlap an accessible route.

Urinal shields may be provided if they do not extend past the front edge of the urinal rim and have a minimum clearance of 29 inches (735 mm) between them (ADAAG 4.18.3).

Flush Controls. Flush controls for urinals must be automatic or operable with one hand. Their operation must not require more than 5 lbf (22.2 N) or tight grasping, pinching, or twisting of the wrist (ADAAG 4.27.4).

For urinals used by children, flush controls should be positioned no higher than 30 inches (760 mm) above the floor (CAH 4.18.4). Controls intended for use by adults must be positioned no higher than 44 inches (1220 mm) above the floor (ADAAG 4.18.4). The Access Board is currently investigating products or design solutions to resolve conflicts between accessibility guidelines for children's urinals and national plumbing codes, which require the flush valve handle to be at least 8-1/2 inches (218 mm) above the urinal (which is usually 27 inches [685 mm] high).

Lavatories and Mirrors

If lavatories (i.e., sinks) and mirrors are provided, at least one of each must comply with the following (ADAAG 4.22.6 and 4.23.6).

Height and Clearances. The counter surface on an accessible lavatory used by children should be no higher than 30 inches (760 mm) above the floor, with at least 27 inches (685 mm) of clearance between the bottom of the lavatory apron and the floor (CAH 4.19.2 and ADAAG, Children's Facilities, 15.8.2). These lavatories must provide a minimum knee clearance measuring 24 inches (610 mm) high, extending a depth of 8 inches (205 mm). In addition, a minimum toe clearance measuring 12 inches (305 mm) high and extending the entire depth of the lavatory must also be provided (ADAAG, Children's Facilities, 15.8.2).

The counter surface of an accessible lavatory intended for use by adults (Figure 4-25) must be no higher than 34 inches (865 mm) above the floor, with at least 29 inches (735 mm) of clearance between the bottom of the lavatory apron and the floor. These lavatories must provide a minimum knee clearance measuring 27 inches (685 mm) high, extending a depth of at least 8 inches (205 mm). In addition, a minimum toe clearance measuring 9 inches (230 mm) high and extending the entire depth of the lavatory must also be provided (ADAAG 4.19.2).

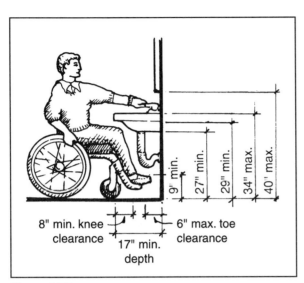

Figure 4-25

8" min. knee clearance

17" min. depth

6" max. toe clearance

9" min.

27" min.

29" min.

34" max.

40' max.

Clear Floor Space. Clear floor space must be provided in front of lavatories to allow a forward approach. Dimensions vary according to the age of the intended user group (see Clear Floor Space in Section II). This space must adjoin or overlap an accessible route and must not extend more than 14 inches (355 mm) beneath lavatories used by children (ADAAG, Children's Facilities, 15.8.3) and 19 inches (485 mm) beneath lavatories used by adults (ADAAG 4.19.3).

Exposed Pipes and Surfaces. Often wheelchair users have impaired sensation in their legs, making them susceptible to burns or cuts without aware-

ness of injury. To protect against injury, hot water and drain pipes under accessible lavatories must be insulated or otherwise configured to protect against contact. In addition, there must be no sharp or abrasive surfaces under accessible lavatories (ADAAG 4.19.4).

Faucets. Accessible lavatory faucets must be controlled electronically or operable with one hand. Their operation must not require more than 5 lbf (22.2 N) or tight grasping, pinching, or twisting of the wrist (ADAAG 4.27.4). Appropriate designs include lever-operated and push-type mechanisms. If self-closing faucet valves are used, they must be set to remain open for at least 10 seconds (ADAAG 4.19.5).

Lavatory Mirrors. In children's environments, the bottom edge of an accessible lavatory mirror should be no higher than 34 inches (865 mm) above the floor (ADAAG, Children's Facilities, 15.8.4). The bottom edge of other accessible lavatory mirrors must be no higher than 40 inches (1015 mm) above the floor (ADAAG 4.19.6).

Full-length mirrors accommodate all users. The top of full-length mirrors in children's environments should measure at least 48 inches (1220 mm) above the floor (CAH 4.19.6). The top of full-length mirrors for adults should measure at least 74 inches (1880 mm) above the floor (ADAAG A4.19.6).

For information on general-purpose sinks, see Sinks, page 63.

Restroom Renovations

Requirements for renovations to an existing facility often vary from those relating to new construction.

Unisex Toilet Room. When making alterations to a facility, it is not always technically feasible to renovate men's and women's toilet rooms to allow for complete access to both. In such instances, providing a "unisex" accessible toilet room may be allowed if at least one per floor is installed in the same area as the existing toilet facilities. Unisex accessible toilet rooms must contain an accessible water closet, an accessible lavatory, and a latch on the door to ensure privacy (ADAAG 4.1.6[3][e][i]).

Stall Design. When remodeling a school facility, the standard accessible stall design is preferred. If use of the standard stall is not technically feasible or would reduce the number of fixtures required by local plumbing codes, alternate stall designs may be substituted (ADAAG 4.1.6[3][e][ii]) (see Toilet Stalls).

Signage. When a toilet room is non-accessible, appropriate signs must be displayed to direct people to the location of the nearest accessible toilet room (ADAAG 4.1.6[3][e][iii]) (see Signage under Moving through the Building).

Amenities

Telephones

Independent use of a public telephone provides everyone at a school facility with a sense of control, social contact, and a method of relaying pertinent information. Accessible public telephones must be available on a school site. Special adaptations such as volume controls must be available and marked with appropriate signs. Telephones should be located away from hallway traffic and public address systems to reduce background noise.

Number of Accessible Phones. When pay, closed-circuit, or other public telephones are available, the number that must be accessible is regulated by guidelines found in ADAAG 4.1.3[17][a] (Table 4-5).

Clear Floor Space. Age-appropriate clear floor space must be provided in front of accessible telephones to allow a forward or side approach by wheelchair users. This space must not be obstructed by bases, enclosures, or fixed seats (ADAAG 4.31.2) (see Clear Floor Space in Section II).

Height of Controls. The controls of accessible telephones must be placed within the reach range of wheelchair users. For telephones used routinely by children, operable parts should be no more than 36 inches (914 mm) above the floor (CAH 4.31.3). The

controls of telephones intended for use solely by adults may be placed higher. For example, if the telephone can be accessed by side reach, operable parts must be no higher than 54 inches (1370 mm) above the floor. If the telephone must be accessed by forward reach, operable parts must be no higher than 48 inches (1220 mm) above the floor (ADAAG 4.31.3) (see Reach Ranges in Section II).

At least one public telephone per floor, however, must meet the requirements for forward reach. An exception is made for exterior telephones: all accessible telephones can be side-reach if dial-tone-first service is available (that is, if a person can reach the operator before inserting coins) (ADAAG 4.1.3[17]).

Telephone Enclosure. For telephones that must be accessed by forward reach, the enclosure must measure at least 30 inches (760 mm) wide, or at least 36 inches wide (915 mm) if the enclosure extends more than 24 inches (610 mm) from the face of the telephone (Figure 4-26). For telephones that can be accessed by side reach, the enclosure must not extend more than 10 inches (255 mm) from the face of the telephone (Figure 4-27) (ADAAG 4.31.2).

To prevent a safety hazard, the bottom edge of the telephone enclosure must meet ADAAG requirements for protruding objects (ADAAG 4.31.2 and Children's Facilities, 15.3) (see Protruding Objects in Section II).

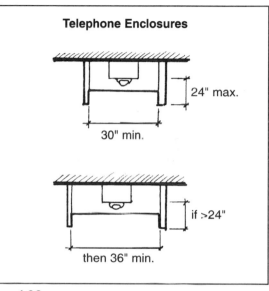

Telephone Enclosures

24" max.
30" min.

if >24"
then 36" min.

Figure 4-26

TABLE 4-5

NUMBER OF TELE-PHONES PROVIDED ON EACH FLOOR	NUMBER OF EACH TYPE OF TELEPHONE REQUIRED TO BE ACCESSIBLE
1 or more single unit	1 per floor
1 bank (two or more adjacent telephones, often installed as a unit)	1 per floor
2 or more banks	1 per bank (the accessible unit may be installed as a single unit in proximity—either visible or with signage—to the bank)

Controls. Telephones must have push-button controls (ADAAG 4.31.6).

Telephone Books. Telephone books, if available, should be located within the reach range of wheel-chair users (ADAAG 4.31.7) (see Reach Ranges in Section II).

Cord Length. The cord from the telephone to the handset must measure at least 29 inches (735 mm) long (ADAAG 4.31.8).

Volume Control. All accessible telephones must be equipped with volume control, allowing a range of sound between 12 and 18 dbA above normal. If the telephone has an automatic reset for volume, the range may exceed the 18 dbA limit (ADAAG 4.31.5). In addition, at least 25 percent of all other public telephones (at least one phone) must have volume control. Phones with volume control must be dispersed throughout the facility (ADAAG 4.1.3[17][b]). Telephones with volume control must be identified with signs depicting a handset with radiating sound waves (Figure 4-28) (ADAAG 4.30.7).

Hearing-Aid Compatibility. All accessible telephones must be hearing-aid compatible (ADAAG 4.31.5). Compatible phones contain a magnetic signal that enhances the sound for people with hearing aids.

Text Telephones. Text telephones, also known as telecommunication display devices (TDDs) and teletypewriters (TTYs), enable people with hearing limitations to communicate through typing and reading.

In new facilities, at least one interior public text telephone must be provided if there are four or more public pay telephones (interior and exterior) on the site, with at least one in an interior location. If a new school facility has a stadium with interior public pay telephones, then at least one of these must be a public text telephone (ADAAG 4.1.3[17][c]).

In renovated facilities, one interior public text telephone is required if the total number of public pay telephones (interior and exterior) increases to four, with at least one in an interior location; or if alterations are made to a public pay telephone in a facility with four or more existing public pay telephones (interior and exterior), with at least one in an interior location (ADAAG 4.1.6[1][e]).

Text telephones used with pay telephones must be permanently affixed within or next to the telephone enclosure. Equivalent facilitation, however, may be provided. For example, a portable text telephone can be stored at the school office and made available when needed. In that instance, at least one pay telephone must accommodate a text telephone (ADAAG 4.31.9).

In new facilities, telephone banks with three or more pay phones must contain one station with a shelf and outlet for text telephone use (ADAAG 4.1.3[17][d]). The shelf must be large enough to accommodate a text telephone and must have a minimum vertical clearance of 6 inches (150 mm) in the area where the text telephone is to be placed (ADAAG 4.31.9[2]). A person must be able to lay a telephone handset flat on the shelf surface.

The International TDD Symbol (Figure 4-29) must be posted to identify the location of text telephones. If a facility has a public text telephone, then all telephone banks without a text telephone must display directions to nearest text telephone (ADAAG 4.30.7[3]).

If the text telephone is not located next to a public telephone, then a sign must provide directions to its location and hours of availability.

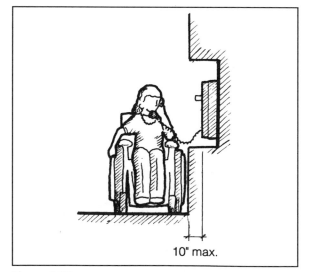

10" max.

Figure 4-27

Drinking Fountains

All children and adults must have access to school drinking fountains or water coolers. Critical design issues to consider include clear floor space to approach the fountain, the positioning of the water spout, and the location and type of control mechanisms.

Number.   In new facilities, each floor must have at least one drinking fountain that is accessible to wheelchair users and at least one that is accessible to people who have difficulty bending their backs or knees. If more than one drinking fountain or water cooler is provided on a floor, at least half must be located along an accessible route and must comply with the following accessibility requirements (ADAAG 4.1.3[10]).

Spout Height.   The spout height of an accessible water fountain for elementary school children should be no greater than 30 inches (762 mm), measured from the spout outlet to the floor (ADAAG, Children's Facilities, 15.5.2). The spout height of other accessible water fountains must be no more than 36 inches (915 mm) above the floor (ADAAG 4.15.2).

Spout Location.   The spout must be at the front of an accessible water fountain, with the water flowing in a path parallel (or nearly so) to the front edge of the unit. If the bowl of the fountain is round or oval, then the spout must be located so that the flow of water is within 3 inches (75 mm) of the front edge of the fountain (ADAAG 4.15.3).

Water Flow.   The flow of water from the spout of an accessible water fountain must rise at least 4 inches (100 mm) to accommodate people who want to fill a container with water (ADAAG 4.15.3).

Controls.   The controls of accessible water fountains must be operable with one hand (for example, push or lever controls). Their operation must not require more than 5 lbf (22.2 N) or tight grasping, pinching, or twisting of the wrist (ADAAG 4.27.4). Controls must be mounted to the front of the fountain, or to the side nearest the front (ADAAG 4.15.4).

Clear Floor Space.   Wall- and post-mounted cantilevered units must have a clear floor space of at least 30 by 48 inches (760 by 1220 mm) to allow a wheelchair user to approach the unit facing forward. The clear floor space should extend no more than 14 inches (305 mm) underneath fountains intended for use by children (ADAAG, Children's Facilities, 15.5.3). Freestanding or built-in units not having a clear space under them must have a clear floor space of at least 30 by 48 inches (760 by 1220 mm) that allows a wheelchair user to make a parallel approach to the unit (Figure 4-30).

Figure 4-28

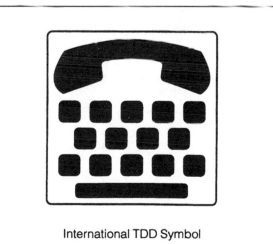

International TDD Symbol

Figure 4-29

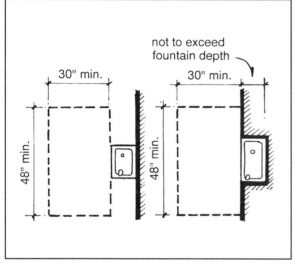

Figure 4-30

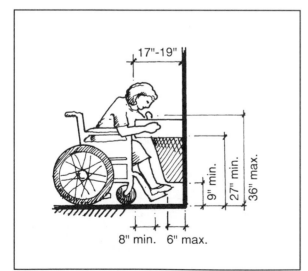

Figure 4-31

Knee Clearance. Accessible wall- and post-mounted cantilevered units (Figure 4-31) must have a clear knee space between the bottom of the apron and the ground at least 27 inches (685 mm) high, 30 inches (760 mm) wide, and 17 to 19 inches (430 to 485 mm) deep (ADAAG 4.15.5).

Proposed rule changes to ADAAG would require accessible cantilevered water fountains intended for use by children to have a clear knee space between the bottom of the apron and the ground at least 24 inches (610 mm) high and 8 inches (205 mm) deep, measured from the fountain's leading edge. The fountains would also need to provide a clear toe space at least 12 inches (305 mm) high, measured from the floor (ADAAG, Children's Facilities, 15.5.3).

Cup Dispensers. Paper cup dispensers should be available where accessible water fountains are unavailable or where water coolers are used. The bottom of the dispenser should be located within the reach range of wheelchair users (see Reach Ranges in Section II). A trash container should be available next to the fountain or cooler without obstructing access.

Vending Machines

Vending machines that provide snacks and beverages should be accessible to everyone. There are three major requirements for vending machines:

- Location along an accessible route (see Accessible Routes in Section III)
- Adequate clear floor space in front of the machine (see Clear Floor Space in Section II)
- Location of controls at an appropriate height (see Reach Ranges in Section II) (ADAAG 5.8, 4.3, and 4.2).

Controls. Push-button selection mechanisms are easier to use than those with pull knobs. Pull-type mechanisms should only require 3 lbf (13.3 N) to operate.

room accessibility

This section provides guidelines for elements found in classrooms and other rooms in school facilities.

Standard Classrooms

The design of classroom settings—where students and teachers spend most of their day—plays an especially important role in accessible education. Aspects of the classroom environment can greatly influence personal attitudes, levels of participation, and quality of work. Classroom elements should be adjustable to meet different uses and needs, which will allow students and teachers the time to focus on educational goals.

Room Arrangement

Classrooms should be arranged so that views of the instructor, audiovisual screens, demonstrations, and exhibits are not obstructed. Students should not have to stretch to look around obstacles. The use of a movable desk or cart for classroom presentations can help to ensure unobstructed views. The placement of an adjustable mirror over the demonstration table will also increase visibility, as will the use of closed-circuit television and well-placed video monitors.

Aisles between work areas and other classroom elements should measure at least 44 inches (1120 mm) wide. This width provides enough space for children using mobility aids to move freely about the room without having to ask others to move chairs, desks, or personal belongings (see Clear Passage Width in Section II).

Work Areas

Uncomfortable work areas can decrease attentiveness and productivity. As a result, work environments should be adjustable to meet a wide range of individual needs and preferences. In newly constructed facilities, at least 5 percent of fixed or built-in seating and tables, and no less than one of each, must comply with ADA guidelines (ADAAG 4.32.1).

Clear Floor Space. If seating is provided for wheelchair users at fixed tables or counters, clear floor space measuring 30 by 48 inches (760 by 1220 mm) must be provided. No more than 14 inches (355 mm) of this space may overlap the area allotted for knee clearance in children's work areas with fixed or built-in seating and tables (ADAAG, Children's Facilities, 15.10.2). The Access Board is considering a proposed rule change for clear floor space to 36 by 48 inches (915 by 1220 mm) (see Clear Floor Space in Section II).

No more than 19 inches (485 mm) of clear floor space may overlap the area allotted for knee clearance in adult work areas (ADAAG 4.32.2).

Knee Clearance. If seating is provided for child wheelchair users at fixed tables or counters, then knee clearance underneath the surface should measure at least 24 inches (610 mm) high, 30 inches (760 mm) wide, and 14 inches (355 mm) deep (ADAAG, Children's Facilities, 15.10.3). Seating provided for adult wheelchair users must have knee clearance at least 27 inches (685 mm) high, 30 inches (760 mm) wide, and 19 inches (485 mm) deep (ADAAG 4.32.3).

Work Surfaces. Work surfaces for child wheelchair users should measure between 26 and 30 inches (660 and 760 mm) above the floor (ADAAG, Children's Facilities, 15.10.4). Work surfaces designed for adult wheelchair users must measure 28 to 34 inches (710 to 865 mm) above the floor (ADAAG 4.32.4).

Adjustable-height surfaces are recommended, since wheelchairs are not manufactured to a standard height. Also, allowing users to adjust the heights of their work areas will better suit the activity at hand. Tasks requiring fine motor control, such as writing, are best accomplished on a surface at elbow level, whereas more forceful movements, such as molding clay, require a surface about 10 inches (255 mm) lower (ADAAG A4.32.4).

Since people often use work surfaces for support when rising from their chairs, surfaces must not tip when pressure is applied to them. Work surfaces should be smooth, with matte or satin finishes to minimize glare. Corners of work surfaces should be rounded to prevent injury.

To accommodate people who use wheelchairs with high armrests, tables with raised leaves should also be available.

Seating. Chairs should be sturdy with height adjustability to allow proper positioning for each student. When seated, individuals should have their feet flat on the floor, with hips and knees at a 90-degree angle. Armrests provide support for people

with mobility or strength limitations and a sense of stability for people with balance difficulties.

Moveable Furniture. Moveable furniture brings flexibility to the classroom. For example, moveable storage units can be used to divide a room into a variety of work spaces, allowing students to work privately in small groups. With moveable furniture, classrooms can be rearranged easily to better suit the constantly changing demands of the curriculum and of the students themselves.

Storage

An integral part of the daily classroom routine involves storing and retrieving items. Conveniently located and easy-to-use storage units benefit everyone. Adjustability is the key to accessible storage, as it enables users to individualize storage systems to meet their personal needs. When a new facility provides fixed or built-in storage—such as cabinets, shelves, closets, and drawers, at least one of each type of storage unit must meet ADA guidelines (ADAAG 4.1.3[12][a]).

Clear Floor Space. Accessible storage areas must have an adjacent clear floor space measuring at least 30 by 48 inches (760 by 1220 mm) (see Clear Floor Space in Section II). Depending on the configuration, this space may allow either a forward or side approach by wheelchair users (ADAAG 4.25.2).

Reach Ranges. Accessible storage areas must be within either a forward or side reach range (ADAAG 4.25.3). Accessible storage areas designed for children should be within a child's reach range (see Reach Ranges in Section II). Clothing racks, hooks, or shelves must not be placed higher than 36 inches (915 mm) above the floor for a side approach (ADAAG, Children's Facilities, 15.9.2). Placement of frequently used items—such as art supplies and writing materials—within this range will enable students to work more independently.

Hardware. Hardware on accessible storage units must be operable with one hand. Their operation must not require more than 5 lbf (22.2 N) to operate or tight grasping, pinching, or twisting of the wrist. Acceptable hardware includes touch latches and U-shaped pulls (ADAAG 4.25.4). Hardware should be placed toward the top edge of lower storage units and toward the bottom edge of upper units.

Cabinets. Cabinets with sliding doors are generally easier to open than those with pull-type, hinged doors, which can become dangerous obstructions when left open. If hinged doors are selected, they should have magnetic door catches, since people are more likely to catch their fingers on spring-type catches.

Cabinet shelves should be stable and secure to allow users to grip them for support or balance.

High, deep shelves are difficult to reach and should be avoided.

Moveable cabinets on casters can be stored under desks and removed to provide knee clearance for wheelchair users. Upper wall cabinets can be placed on brackets, making them readily adjustable to different heights.

It is recommended that toe space under cabinets should be provided to allow closer access for wheelchair users.

Closets. Closets should have well-constructed bi-fold, pocket, or sliding doors. Bi-fold doors are often preferred because they stack flush against the wall and have a narrow and easy-to-operate design. They also allow full access to the storage closet and do not require a large floor area or floor tracks.

Lockers. Lockers should have built-in combination dials with large, clear numerals on a contrasting background. Locks and latches should be operable with one hand. For stacked locker units, locks and latches should be placed toward the top edge of lower lockers and toward the bottom edge of upper lockers.

It is recommended that lockers at wall intersections should be at least 24 inches (610 mm) from the intersecting wall. This space allows for maneuvering and side-positioning by a person using a mobility aid (consistent with ADAAG 4.13.6).

Floor Surfaces

The need to plan each step diligently is a constant concern for people with balance difficulties, weak lower extremities, incoordination, or painful joints. As a result, floor surfaces should be carefully selected to re-inforce safety and accessibility. Walking surfaces should be slip-resistant, firm, level, and easy to maintain. Surfaces that may hinder wheelchair movement—such as thick carpeting, sand, gravel, brick, and flagstone—should be avoided.

Carpeting. Carpeting should be low-profile and tightly woven, such as level-loop, textured-loop, level-cut, or level cut/uncut pile carpets. Carpets and rugs should be secured firmly to the floor. To prevent tripping hazards, fringes around rugs should not measure more than 1/2 inch (13 mm) long, and frayed carpet edges should be bound together.

The recommended maximum carpet pile height in children's environments is 1/4 inch (6 mm) (CAH 4.5.3). Carpet pile in other environments must not be more than 1/2 inch (13 mm) high (ADAAG 4.5.3). When possible, carpets should be installed without pads. Pads add extra height and sponginess, which can hinder wheelchair movement and create problems for people with weak lower extremities.

Other Surfaces. Non-glazed ceramic tile, hardwood floors with non glossy finishes, and other slip-resistant floor surfaces are also suitable for classroom settings. Vinyl tiles are preferred to vinyl-sheet flooring because individual squares are easier to replace when damaged. Thick padding should not use used with vinyl-sheet flooring because mobility aids or sharp tools can easily gouge padded surfaces.

Floor Patterns. Floor patterns should be muted. Complicated designs can hinder the functional abilities of some users. For example, they may be tripping hazards for people with diminished depth perception.

Changes in Level. Level changes on floor surfaces, such as where two different floor coverings adjoin, must meet the following requirements.

- Level changes up to 1/4 inch (6 mm) may be vertical and without edge treatment.

- Level changes between 1/4 and 1/2 inch (6 and 13 mm) must be beveled with a slope not greater than 1:2.

- Level changes greater than 1/2 inch (13 mm) must be ramped (ADAAG 4.5.2).

Visual Cues. Coverings of distinct tactile and visual character can provide orientation cues. The use of varied colors and materials can help individuals to distinguish different parts of a room.

Lighting, HVAC, and Acoustics

Although specialized professionals should oversee the design and control of these environmental systems, the following guidelines highlight several key considerations.

General Lighting. Surface-mounted light fixtures are preferred to recessed fixtures, which trap sound. Similarly, face panels for fluorescent lights are acoustically reflective and are preferred to open, egg-crate panels because the resulting sound reflection enhances the room's acoustics.

Natural light can be a great asset to any space, so long as controls are present to reduce glare and unwanted heat gain.

Task Lighting. Task lighting provides supplemental illumination that can be adjusted to meet personal needs and preferences. Enough electrical outlets should be installed around a room to allow for flexibility in task lighting.

Electrical Outlets. Electrical outlets should be installed at accessible locations throughout a room. They should be available near individual work areas where students may wish to use tape recorders, personal readers, and task lighting. Pull-down outlets can be very useful, because they avoid the hazard posed by trailing electrical cords on the floor.

Room Temperature. A room's ambient temperature can affect student attentiveness and productivity. Cooler temperatures are conducive for quiet work; warmer temperatures can cause drowsiness. Classroom thermostats should be set at 72 degrees Fahrenheit or lower; in areas of physical activity, thermostats should be set at even lower temperatures. A zoned temperature control system allows individual temperature adjustments in different areas of a facility.

Mechanical Noise. To reduce background noise, the mechanical rooms for heating and ventilating systems must be located away from classrooms and other designated "quiet" areas. Mechanical noise can be extremely distracting and may prevent students from learning, especially those children with hearing limitations. A mechanical systems engineer or physical plant employee should be consulted to find ways to control noise and vibrations from HVAC systems, lighting ballasts, projector fans, and other equipment.

Background Noise and Reverberation. Acoustic environments should be designed to reduce interference, background noise, and reverberation (echo). A minimum threshold of acoustical absorption should be assured in each room to facilitate cognitive functions and communication. Floor carpeting can provide the most cost-effective means for acoustical absorption. The use of window treatments, carpets, wall hangings, and upholstered furniture can also help absorb noise. Fabric-paneled screens can be used to create individual study carrels for students easily distracted by background noise.

Windows

Windows requiring a twist, push, or slide motion to operate—such as casement, awning, or slide windows—are preferred since these movements are easier to perform than the push-up and pull-down motion needed to operate a double-hung window. Opening or closing a window should not require more than 5 lbf (22.2 N) (ADAAG A4.12.2).

While exposure to natural light is essential for emotional and physical health, direct sunlight can create difficult visual conditions in classrooms and other areas. Adjustable window treatments, such as blinds or drapes, allow people to control the amount of light entering a room and eliminate glare or visual distractions. Window controls and locks should be operable with one closed fist.

Classroom Equipment

Chalkboards. It is easier to write on a slanted board than on one placed flat against a wall. Therefore, chalkboards should angle outward 3 to 6 inches (75 to 150 mm) at the bottom. Brown or green chalkboards are preferable to black chalkboards because they reflect less glare and, therefore, are easier to read.

Computers.   Personal computers play an increasingly important role in primary and secondary education. The rise in computer-related injuries, such as carpal tunnel syndrome, requires that careful attention be given to the design of computer work stations. Adjustability is a key concern when arranging individual work areas. The following factors must be considered: chair type, knee space, height of the keyboard and video display, location of the document holder and assistive devices, and clear floor space around the work area.

Carts.   Lightweight carts with easy-to-maneuver wheels should be available for transporting books and equipment.

Sinks

Use of a sink is often an important aspect of classroom activities, especially when cleaning up is required. As a result, at least one sink in the classroom must be accessible. Sinks for classrooms use similar guidelines to those for sinks in toilet rooms (see Lavatories and Mirrors in the previous section for allowable sink heights, knee clearances, clear floor space dimensions, faucets, and exposed pipes and surfaces underneath sinks).

Sink Depth.   According to current guidelines, the bowl of a sink must not be deeper than 6-1/2 inches (165 mm) (ADAAG 4.24.4). A deeper bowl will not allow room for adequate knee clearance. Also, wheelchair users may find it difficult to see or use the bottom of a deep sink. However, CAH recommendations regarding the rim height and knee clearance for sinks used by children limit a sink's bowl depth to 5-1/2 inches (138 mm). In fact, some states currently require that mounting heights for sinks serving young children be 24 to 26 inches (610 to 660 mm). The Access Board is currently investigating product or design solutions that will provide sinks with 24-inch (610 mm) knee clearance and 30-inch (760 mm) rim height that are also usable by young, ambulatory children.

Art Rooms

Active participation is vital to art education. The design of an art room must ensure that all students can take part in class activities to the fullest extent of their skills. Student wheelchair users, for example, cannot learn the process of photography until they can enter the darkroom to use enlargers, sinks, and other photographic equipment.

Lighting.   Due to the visual nature of art, ample lighting is essential. Window treatments should be available to adjust the amount of light and reduce glare. Task lighting should also be available.

Ventilation.   Good ventilation is essential for removing unpleasant fumes from paint, adhesive, and other art supplies. Such fumes can be particularly irritating for people with respiratory problems.

Sinks.   At least one sink in an art room must be accessible (see Sinks under Standard Classrooms).

Art Displays.   Display areas should be accessible to allow close inspection of artwork. Space should also be allotted for display of touchable artwork. Allowing students, especially those with visual limitations, to appreciate art through the sense of touch has become an important teaching method (see Clear Floor Space and Reach Ranges in Section II).

Storage.   Storage is an important feature in art rooms due to the assortment of materials and supplies used. Peg boards for hanging tools at reachable heights provide an excellent storage system in art rooms (see Storage under Standard Classrooms).

Darkroom.   Darkrooms must be accessible to wheelchair users. Darkroom doors must have at least 32 inches (815 mm) of clear passage. Enlargers and other equipment must be located no higher than 48 inches (1220 mm) from the floor, with adequate clear floor space for maneuvering. Sinks must be accessible. Darkrooms have special ventilation requirements due to the nature of the chemicals used when developing negatives or prints.

Equipment and Tools. Adjustable-height easels and printing presses, extra-large chalk and crayons, and tools with large handles allow all students and staff to participate in art projects. A cart is useful for transporting supplies between storage shelves, work tables, drying areas, and display cases.

Music Rooms

Besides developing individual skills and discipline, music classes provide learning opportunities in a group setting. Training in vocal and instrumental music can be an enriching experience for all students.

Access to Raised Areas or Tiers. A music room often consists of raised areas or tiers to allow full view of the conductor and the grouping of performers into sections. Access to each part of the room is essential for the full integration of each student (see Assembly Areas later in this section for guidelines on adequate clear floor space and width of floor levels for accommodating people using wheelchairs, mobility aids, or guide dogs).

Lighting. Available task lighting for reading music should be lightweight, portable, and battery-

operated (see Lighting, HVAC, and Acoustics under Standard Classrooms).

Lockers. Accessible lockers should be available within or near the music room to provide secure storage for instruments, music stands, and folders (see Storage under Standard Classrooms).

Home Economics Rooms

Home economics courses teach important basic life skills such as cooking and sewing. Accessibility to these classrooms—and to the basic knowledge imparted in them—enables all students to lead more independent lives.

General Requirements

Lighting. Available task lighting for sewing and other detailed work should be lightweight, portable, and battery-operated (see Lighting, HVAC, and Acoustics under Standard Classrooms).

Noise Level. A home economics room—with appliances being run, students working on projects, and teachers providing guidance—can be quite noisy. Posters, fabric wall hangings, and window treatments will help absorb class noise.

Clear Floor Space. Adequate clear floor space must exist between sewing machine, tables and

other work areas. Aisles should be at least 44 inches (1120 mm) wide.

Work Tables. Work tables should have a minimum clearance of 32 inches (815 mm) between table legs. This clearance must not be obstructed by bracing, skirts, fascias, or table bases. Pedestal-base tables with low, tapered bases are recommended for wheelchair users because they eliminate the obstruction often created by table legs. Such tables should provide leg room at least 19 inches (485 mm) deep and have a surface diameter of 42 to 48 inches (1065 to 1220 mm).

A portable raised leaf allows tables to be modified for use by people using larger wheelchairs.

The height-adjustable leaf should measure 10 inches (255 mm) in length and project 6 inches (150 mm) beyond the edge of the table.

Counters. Lower work surfaces are important in food labs because of the many types of work that take place there. Whereas the optimum height for writing is near a seated person's elbow, the optimum height for heavy manual work such as rolling dough is approximately 10 inches (255 mm) lower. At least one lower (or adjustable-height) counter should be available, measuring no more than 30 inches (760 mm) high and providing a knee clearance at least 27 inches (685 mm) high, 36 inches (915 mm) wide, and 19 inches (485 mm) deep.

Counters should be continuous and heat-resistant to allow people to slide hot cooking dishes rather than lift them. Corners on all tables and counters must be rounded for safety.

Living Room Area. If a living room area is provided, armchairs should be provided for students with low muscle tone, weak muscles, mobility limitations, and low stamina. Task lighting should be available for reading.

Fire Safety. Because fires can arise quickly while cooking, each food lab must have appropriate equipment and materials to extinguish fires. A lightweight, portable fire extinguisher should be provided at each workstation used by people who may find it difficult to reach the room fire extinguisher.

Storage. Peg boards for hanging tools at reachable heights provide an excellent storage system in a home economics room (see Storage under Standard Classrooms).

Appliances

Stoves. A stovetop mounted onto a low-height counter allows seated individuals to participate fully in the cooking process. This range must be flush with the adjoining counter so students can easily and safely slide pots on and off its surface. There are no provisions for knee clearance underneath the stovetop, as it is extremely dangerous to sit with one's legs directly underneath boiling pots and pans. For safety reasons, a stovetop should have staggered or offset burners, so a person can use the back burners without reaching over the front ones. Similarly, controls should be located at the front or side edge of the appliance, so a person does not have to reach over the burners to adjust the controls.

Ovens. Wall-mounted ovens are often easier to operate because they do not require people to bend their backs or knees. They also allow wheelchair users to position themselves closely. The oven door should open on side hinges. A pull-out board beneath the oven provides a convenient place for preparing food or resting hot dishes. Oven controls should be located between 40 and 48 inches (1015 and 1220 mm) from the floor.

Exhaust Fans. Controls for exhaust fans should be located on the apron of the counter so that seated individuals can access them.

Refrigerators. Although the ADA guidelines do not address refrigerators or freezers, the American National Standards Institute recommends that 50 percent of the storage capacity of refrigerators or freezers be located within standard reach ranges (see Reach Ranges in Section II). Also, the refrigerator door should open a full 180 degrees, which allows easier access to refrigerator contents by people who use a mobility aid.

Washers and Dryers. Front-loading washers and dryers are easier to use. Machine controls should also be located on the front, with large numbers and letters in contrasting colors to assist people with low visual ability.

Utensils. All eating and serving utensils should be symmetrical for use by either right- or left-handed people. They should have large-diameter handles to allow for an easier grasp. Four-pronged forks are preferable, since three-pronged forks are longer and more difficult to balance and manipulate.

Small, lightweight pitchers with attached lids allow use with one hand. Textured glassware is easier to grip than smooth-surfaced items. Cups should have large, easy-to-grasp handles and large bases to prevent them from being knocked over easily. Straws should be available for people who may have difficulty lifting and drinking from cups.

Science Labs

Lessons in science are enhanced tremendously by hands-on experiments and demonstrations. These activities, however, often require the use of equipment and supplies (such as glassware, burners, and chemicals that are harmful alone or in combination with others) that pose safety hazards. Care must be taken to modify work areas, equipment, and procedures to provide students the greatest degree of independence with the lowest potential for accidents.

Every user of a science lab must have easy access to safety equipment and supplies. Emergency laboratory procedures must be developed, evaluated, and practiced on a routine basis, a process that requires a thorough understanding of current local safety codes and appropriate federal standards. Students in the science lab should always be familiar with these procedures and work under the close supervision of an instructor.

Ventilation. Ventilation standards in science labs are strictly regulated because many chemicals are toxic, depending on type, quantity, and use in combinations. Consequently, lab safety engineers must be consulted in the design of ventilation systems for classroom use. Science experiments must be limited to those for which safe ventilation and safe working conditions (as determined by local, state, and federal regulations) can be provided.

Interior Finishes. Interior finishes must be impervious to the chemicals commonly used in science labs, such as acids and those with strong coloring agents.

Lab Stations

Accessible lab stations must be positioned as closely as possible to the accessible path of egress from the room to assist individuals who may have difficulty evacuating in an emergency. A number of factors should be considered when locating accessible lab stations: safety, proximity to shared equipment, conflicts with general traffic patterns, wheelchair maneuvering dimensions, and the ability of others to move around a wheelchair user.

Accessible Lab Stations. A section of a lab station should be lowered to an appropriate work height for wheelchair users—30 to 36 inches (760 to 915 mm) from the floor. If the lab station has an apron or storage units beneath its surface, these obstructions should be removed to provide knee clearance appropriate to the age of intended users. For example, knee clearance for older children in wheelchairs should measure at least 27 inches (685 mm) high, 36 inches (915 mm) wide, and 14 inches (355 mm) deep. Clear floor space must be provided in front of the lab station. Modular work stations that are rail-hung without the use of table legs and that consist of free-standing units provide additional maneuvering space for people using mobility aids.

If a lab station needs to be adapted for wheelchair access, a drop-leaf extension should be installed. The utilities should be moved forward and within easy reach of users to compensate for the additional depth of the lab station. The extension should be installed where sufficient aisle width exists to accommodate general foot traffic.

Seating. An adjustable-height armchair can be provided for individuals who prefer to transfer from a wheelchair. This type of chair can be useful for people who have problems with standing, balance, stamina, or use of their hands. For these individuals, fine motor skills can be enhanced significantly when working in a seated rather than standing position.

Sinks. At least one sink in a science lab must be accessible (see Sinks under Standard Classrooms).

Controls. Controls on supply lines must be operable with a closed fist and no more than 5 lbf (22.2 N). Lever handles and blade handles are suitable choices. Controls must not be positioned more than 12 to 18 inches (305 to 455 mm) from the edge of the work surface to be within easy reach.

Storage. Adaptable storage should be provided next to and beneath lab stations. Appropriate storage designs for lab stations include multiple compartments, cylindrical storage on "Lazy Susans," and cabinets on casters that can be moved when clear floor space is needed.

Safety Equipment

Safety equipment is an important element of classroom experiments. All users of the science lab should follow standard safety guidelines.

Protective Wear. During experiments, teachers and students should always wear safety goggles with side shields. Heavy rubber aprons to protect against damage from spilled chemicals should be available for seated individuals and those with sensory limitations. Protective wear should be kept in accessible storage areas (see Storage under Standard Classrooms).

Eyewash Station. Eyewash solution and written instructions for its use should be at a station that is 40 to 48 inches (1015 to 1220 mm) high. Eyewash should also be provided at the lab areas of individuals who cannot reach the eyewash station easily. At these lab areas, the eyewash dispensing device must be placed in an accessible location. Another approach is to attach a flexible hose to the dispensing device so that a seated person can use it.

Emergency Showers. Accessible lab stations should be close to emergency showers. A pull chain should be attached to the lab's emergency shower apparatus. To be within easy reach, the end of the chain should hang no more than 40 to 48 inches (1015 to 1220 mm) from the floor. In addition to a standard lab hose, there should be a means of "hosing-down" individuals who find it difficult to get to the standard shower apparatus.

Fire Extinguishers. Local regulations govern the required placement and number of fire extinguishers in classrooms and school labs. Lightweight portable fire extinguishers should be provided at the lab stations for people who find it difficult to reach the room fire extinguisher.

On-and-Off Lights. All equipment should have large, easily visible, on-and-off indicator lights. This visual cue can serve as a necessary source of information for people with low vision or hearing ability and it can serve as a reminder to all students that a piece of equipment is in operation.

Gas Jets. In addition to the standard "hiss" sound made by an open gas jet, an odorant should be added to the gas supply so people with hearing difficulties can detect the presence of gas. An unusual smell can be more effective in alerting people in a noisy room.

Signage. Well-placed signs should identify the location of safety equipment (for example, emergency showers, eyewash stations, and first-aid kits).

Emergency Lighting. Emergency lighting is recommended in case of power outages. This safety measure is particularly helpful for people with hearing limitations who rely on visual cues for directions during emergencies.

Greenhouse and Gardens

Gardening can provide valuable educational experiences. Students learn how to take care of living things as they observe developmental changes and growth. Horticulture, due to its multisensory nature, allows meaningful involvement by all students. For example, a student with visual limitations can feel the soil, touch the shoots of a young seedling, smell the moisture in the ground, and enjoy the scents of different plants.

Activities such as mixing soils, planting seeds, pruning, and watering can be adapted easily to allow participation by students at all functional skill levels. In addition, through the use of raised beds or containers, planting areas can be placed at various levels to allow easier access for people with mobility limitations.

Outdoor Gardens. If a school has an outdoor garden area, then an accessible path should be included in its design. The path's surface should be level, secure, and free from debris or obstacles. The path should measure at least 48 inches (1220 mm) wide.

Work Surfaces. Work surfaces must be accessible for students and staff who use wheelchairs or who prefer to work while seated. Clear floor space allowance, adequate reach ranges, and proper table heights are important features of accessible work surfaces.

Flower Boxes. Flower boxes for use by young children should not be higher than 22 inches (560 mm) from the ground. In no case should they be located more than 36 inches (915 mm) from the ground. Clear ground space must be provided around accessible flower boxes to allow wheelchair access.

To increase the sensory experience for all students, colorful flowers and foliage with a variety of scents should be planted.

Storage Bins. Portable soil storage bins that can be pulled, pushed, or rolled should be provided in a gardening area.

Assembly Areas

Assembly areas such as the school auditorium provide places for people to come together for special performances and presentations. Whether as performers, speakers, or audience members, all users of a school facility must have access to these areas, including the stage and dressing rooms. All members of the audience should have clear views

and access to assistive listening systems when necessary.

An accessible route should connect the stage, arena floor, dressing rooms, locker rooms, wheelchair seating locations, and other applicable areas.

Aisles must meet standard space requirements of wheelchair users (see Section II). Handrails should be placed along walls beside aisles to assist people who need support and balance.

Accessible Seating

Assembly areas with fixed seating must provide wheelchair-accessible seating (ADAAG 4.1.3[19]). The following table lists the required number of wheelchair locations for an assembly area (ADAAG 4.1.3[19][a]).

TABLE 5.1

SEATING CAPACITY	NUMBER OF REQUIRED WHEELCHAIR LOCATIONS
4 to 25	1
26 to 50	2
51 to 300	4
301 to 500	6
more than 500	6 plus 1 additional space per each 100 additional seats

Size of Wheelchair Locations. Wheelchair locations must measure at least 33 inches (840 mm) wide; 36 inches (915 mm) is preferred. The required length of wheelchair locations depends on the type of access provided. If the wheelchair location is accessed from the front or rear, then it must measure at least 48 inches (1220 mm) long (Figure 5-1). If the wheelchair location is accessed from the side, it must measure at least 60 inches (1525 mm) long (Figure 5-2) (ADAAG 4.33.2). Locations should be designed so that two wheelchair users can sit next to each other (ADAAG A4.33.2).

Placement of Wheelchair Locations. Wheelchair locations must be placed along an accessible route that can serve as a means of egress. Ideally, wheelchair locations should be integrated into areas of fixed seats to provide wheelchair users the same set of viewing and pricing options as other people (ADAAG A4.33.3). When a wheelchair location is not being used by wheelchair users, removable chairs may be installed there.

An exception is made for wheelchair locations designated for bleachers, balconies, and other areas where slopes are steeper than 5 percent. In those cases, alternate seating with equivalent viewing may be clustered on levels with accessible egress. It must be noted, however, that "equivalent" viewing may be difficult to accomplish. In addition, the number of seats available in these clusters is often limited, and wheelchair users who sit in such sections are often separated from other spectators.

Accompanying Seating. At least one fixed seat must be installed next to each wheelchair location for use by the wheelchair user's companion (ADAAG 4.33.3). To enable families or small groups to sit together, portable chairs may be used to provide additional seating.

Floor Surfacing. The floor surface of wheelchair locations must be level (with a slope no greater than 1:50) and firm (ADAAG 4.33.4).

Adaptable Aisle Seats. Some wheelchair users prefer to transfer from their wheelchairs to fixed seats in an assembly area. To accommodate these individuals, at least 1 percent of all fixed seats, and no less than one seat, must be aisle seats without an armrest or with a removable or folding armrest on the aisle side. Adaptable aisle seats are not required to be on a level surface. Signs must identify adaptable aisle seats, and additional informational signs are required at the ticket office to inform people of the availability of adaptable aisle seating (ADAAG 4.1.3[19]).

Storage space for wheelchairs should be provided adjacent to adaptable aisle seats or in a nearby alcove. Wheelchairs should be kept near their users and must not obstruct the path of travel. This clear space also benefits individuals accompanied by guide dogs.

Seating for People with Braces, Crutches, or Lower Limb Prostheses. To improve comfort for people with these mobility aids, seats with 24 inches (610 mm) of knee clearance between the front edge of the seat and the seats in front may be provided.

Assistive Listening Systems

An assistive listening system or accommodations for a portable sound system must be provided in auditoriums and other places where audible communication is an integral part of the function and enjoyment of the area. The listening device must be a permanently installed assistive listening system if the room accommodates at least 50 people and has fixed seating, or if the room has audio-amplification systems and fixed seating.

If the room does not meet either of these criteria, there are two courses of action to take: either install a permanent system, or install adequate electrical outlets or other supplementary wiring to support a portable assistive listening system (ADAAG 4.1.3[19][b]).

Figure 5-1

Figure 5-2

Number of Receivers. The minimum number of listening system receivers that must be provided in a facility equals 4 percent of the total number of seats, but never less than two receivers (ADAAG 4.1.3[19][b]).

Location of Listening Systems. People with hearing limitations often rely on people's gestures and facial expressions to understand what is being said. As a result, when the assistive listening system serves individual fixed seats, these seats must be located within 50 feet (15 m) of the stage and provide a complete view of the stage (ADAAG 4.33.6).

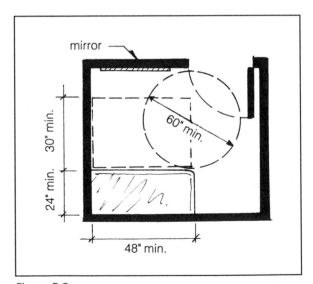

Figure 5-3

Many people with hearing limitations are more adept at reading lips than sign language. Seating close to the stage that also allows a complete view of stage performers should be provided in addition to the presence of on-stage sign language interpreters.

Signage. Signage that includes the International Symbol of Access for Hearing Loss is required if the assembly area has permanently installed assistive listening systems (see Telephones in Section IV) (ADAAG 4.1.3[19][b]).

Stage Area and Dressing Rooms

Designers should remember that wheelchair users may be performers as well as spectators, so access to the stage and dressing rooms is essential. Also, some events may require audience members to come up to the stage or enter the backstage area.

At least 5 percent of the dressing rooms, but never less than one in each cluster of dressing rooms, must be accessible and comply with ADA guidelines (ADAAG 4.1.3[21]).

Turning Space. If a dressing room has a swinging or sliding door, it must have a clear floor space measuring 60 inches (1525 mm) in diameter to allow a wheelchair user to make a 180-degree turn (Figure 5-3). The dressing room door must not swing into

this turning space. No turning space, however, is required if the entrance consists of a curtain that opens at least 32 inches (815 mm) wide and if enough clear floor space exists to allow a wheelchair user to enter and maneuver within the dressing room (ADAAG 4.35.2).

Doors. Doors to accessible dressing rooms must be accessible (ADAAG 4.35.3) (see Doors in Section IV).

Benches. Each accessible dressing room must provide a bench that meets the following criteria (ADAAG 4.35.4).

- The bench must measure 24 by 48 inches (610 by 1220 mm) and must be securely attached to the longer wall.
- It must be mounted 17 to 19 inches (430 to 485 mm) above the floor.
- Clear floor space must be provided alongside the bench to allow a wheelchair user to make a parallel transfer onto the bench.
- The bench must be structurally sound and able to withstand 250 lbf (1112 N).

Mirrors. If mirrors are provided in any dressing rooms, a full-length mirror must be installed in each accessible dressing room. The mirror must measure at least 18 by 54 inches (460 by 1370 mm) and allow use whether seated or standing (see Lavatories and Mirrors in Section IV) (ADAAG 4.35.5).

Warning Strip. A 30-inch (760 mm) wide textured warning strip should be placed along the edge of the stage to warn people on stage about any sudden drop-offs.

Stage Lighting. To ensure that expressions and gestures of speakers and performers are clearly visible, stage lighting must be arranged to avoid shadows on hands, faces, and torsos. Improved stage lighting assists people with limited vision, who may be sensitive to glare, and individuals who depend on physical gestures and expressions for enhanced language comprehension.

When sign language interpreters are on stage, they should stand or sit to the side of or directly behind the person speaking. A non-glare light should be focused directly on the interpreter.

Equipment Height. Equipment such as marker boards, chalkboards, and fixed microphones should be adjustable in height to accommodate performers and speakers of various heights.

Ticket Booths

When ticket booths are provided, they must be located along an accessible route, preferably near the auditorium or gymnasium, where most events

requiring tickets take place. Spectators should be able to approach the booth easily, purchase a ticket, and move directly to the seating area.

Part of the main counter must be accessible. The accessible portion must measure at least 36 inches (915 mm) long and no more than 36 inches (915 mm) high. If these dimensions are not feasible, a nearby auxiliary counter no more than 36 inches (915 mm) high must be provided, or an alternate method of sales must be provided (ADAAG 7.2). The 36-inch counter is low enough for children, people of short stature, and wheelchair users to make transactions easily. The purpose of this guideline is to ensure dignity and allow everyone the opportunity to purchase a ticket without special treatment.

Gymnasiums

Athletic facilities are often the site of school and community programs, as well as sports events. For this reason, indoor athletic facilities, including locker rooms and auxiliary rooms, must provide full access to all spectators and participants in these events. The gymnasium must connect to the school's main accessible route. A separate accessible route to outdoor playing fields should also be provided.

Lighting. Lighting is essential for people with hearing and sight limitations to see facial expressions and read lips. Proper illumination of interpreters is also essential.

Sound System. A high-quality audio amplification system is important in obtaining static-free sound.

Basketball Hoops. Basketball hoops with adjustable heights enable wheelchair users and younger children to participate in games.

Bleachers. Bleachers should be constructed with a gradual slope and secure handrails at the steps.

Floor Coverings. Gymnasium floors must have a slip-resistant finish.

Locker Rooms. Aisles between rows of lockers must measure at least 36 inches (915 mm) wide, which allows for only a side approach by wheelchair users. A better solution would be to vary the size of aisle widths, with 36 inches (915 mm) as the minimum width and 48 inches (1220 mm) as the preferred width. In any case, a clear floor space measuring 36 by 48 inches (915 by 1220 mm) must be provided at lockers designated for wheelchair users.

At least one group of lockers should not have benches in front of them. A padded, 18-inch (455 mm) high dressing table should be substituted for people needing extra support while dressing, such as those with mobility aids or balance problems.

The table should be positioned with one or two edges against a wall for additional support. For wheelchair access, a 60-by-60 inch (1525 by 1525 mm) wheelchair turning space is recommended.

Lockers should comply with the guidelines outlined in Storage under Standard Classrooms. Restrooms and showers must comply with the guidelines presented in Restrooms in Section IV.

Locker rooms should have at least one full-length mirror, which can be used by a sitting or standing person.

Shelves, clothing racks, and hooks should not be more than 36 inches (915 mm) from the floor in children's environments and 48 inches (1220 mm) from the floor for other facilities. Opening and closing mechanisms, such as those that slide or use a lever, should be operable with a closed fist.

Cafeterias

School cafeterias provide a central setting for meals, socializing, study sessions, and meetings. Accessible cafeterias allow students to function independently and efficiently. All newly constructed dining areas must be accessible, including outdoor or raised seating areas (ADAAG 5.4). In building renovations where the entire dining area cannot be altered, accessible areas must provide the same decor and services as the rest of the area and be able to support general use.

Room Arrangement. All cafeteria aisles should measure 44 to 48 inches (1120 to 1220 mm) wide. Narrower aisles pose a safety hazard, particularly for students carrying trays of food.

Objects such as trash receptacles must not obstruct the path of travel. Such objects should be visually marked with bright colors to warn of possible hazards (see Protruding Objects in Section II).

The arrangement of tables and chairs should include enough turning space for wheelchair users to make 180-degree turns (see Wheelchair Turning Space in Section II).

Raised Platform

Raised Platform. When the cafeteria provides a raised platform for ceremonies or performances, access for people unable to negotiate stairs can be achieved with a ramp or platform lift. The open edges of a raised platform must be protected by a curb or the placement of tables along the edge (ADAAG 5.7).

Serving Areas

Food-service lines must meet standard guidelines for clear passage width (see Clear Passage Width in Section II).

Tray Slides. Tray slides used primarily by children should be no higher than 30 inches (760 mm) above the floor (CAH 5.2). Tray slides in faculty and staff dining areas must be no higher than 34 inches (865 mm) above the floor (ADAAG 5.5).

Tray slides should run continuously from tray storage bins to cashier stations. This arrangement enables students to slide trays along a surface and reduces their chances of dropping their trays.

Food selections should be placed within 15 inches (380 mm) of the leading edge of the tray slide to allow access by wheelchair users (CAH 5.2).

Self-Service Shelves. At least half of the self-service shelves in food-service lines must fall within the reach range of wheelchair users (ADAAG 5.5). All self-service shelves and dispensers in tableware and condiment areas must fall within the reach range of wheelchair users (ADAAG 5.6) (see Reach Ranges in Section II).

Utensils and food supplies should be stored vertically at a convenient height for all users. Self-service drink dispensers should allow a container to rest on a level surface while being filled.

Vending Machines. The requirements for vending machines are discussed in Section IV.

Dining Areas

If a school cafeteria has fixed or built-in seating or tables, at least 5 percent, but not less than one of each, must be accessible. When possible, accessible seating and tables must be interspersed throughout the cafeteria to provide a variety of seating options for individuals with disabilities. To promote interaction within the school community, a mix of seating options for all people would include tables of different shapes and with different seating capabilities and configurations.

Dining area guidelines are similar to guidelines discussed earlier for kitchens in home economics rooms, including dimensions for clear floor space, knee clearance, table heights, seating, and utensils (see also Work Areas under Standard Classrooms).

Libraries and Media Centers

For many children with disabilities, visiting the school library or media center is their favorite activity of the day. Large-print books, computers, audiovisual material, and text talkers enable them to engage fully in all types of learning. As a result, the design of these facilities will need to accommodate a variety of users.

Circulation. Pathways must be designed so library users will not have to walk through rows of tables or seated readers to access the bookshelves. Aisles between bookshelves, furniture, card catalogues, and other displays must be at least 36 inches (914 mm) wide, although widths of 42 to 44 inches (1065 to 1120 mm) are recommended (ADAAG 8.5).

Although clear, unobstructed open space is a key feature of accessible design, seats should be positioned no more than 40 to 50 feet (12 to 15 m) apart to accommodate people who have difficulty walking long distances and need to sit frequently.

Reading and Study Areas.   If fixed tables or seating are provided, at least 5 percent of them, and no less than one table or seat, must be accessible (ADAAG 4.32) (see Work Areas under Standard Classrooms).

Stackable chairs are recommended because they require less storage space and can be removed to provide space for wheelchairs or other purposes.

Study carrels can be suspended from wall tracks to eliminate protruding table legs and braces, which can be obstacles to wheelchair users.

Reference Areas.   The maximum height at which card catalogues and reading material for use by younger children should be placed is 36 inches (914 mm) (CAH 8.4). These items must not be placed higher than 48 inches (1220 mm) for adult users (see Reach Ranges in Section II).

A lateral filing system for card catalogues is preferred to a vertical system because the backs of vertical file drawers are often difficult to access.

Many library catalogues are now provided on computers. Computers, however, are only useful if students and staff can use them easily and independently. Clear instructions should be located in a well-lighted place next to the computer terminal. Auditory and large-print directions should be available upon request.

Media Rooms.   Media rooms allow people with visual limitations to use assistive devices such as enlargers, tape recorders, special light fixtures, and talking calculators without distracting other library users. To prevent distractions, these rooms must be soundproofed.

Check-out Areas.   In elementary schools, the maximum counter height at check-out areas should not exceed 30 inches (762 mm) from the floor (CAH 8.3). Areas of check-out counters used primarily by adults must be no more than 36 inches (915 mm) above the floor for a distance at least 36 inches (915 mm) long (ADAAG 8.3).

The check-out counter, which is often busy, noisy, and active, should be kept away from reading and study areas.

If security gates or other means of traffic control exist at an exit, they must be accessible (ADAAG 8.3).